JESUS ★★★★★★★★★★★ WAS A ★★★★★★★★★★★
COUNTRY BOY

LIFE LESSONS
on Faith, Fishing,
& Forgiveness

★

CLAY WALKER

HOWARD BOOKS
A DIVISION OF SIMON & SCHUSTER, INC.
New York · Nashville · London · Toronto · Sydney · New Delhi

Howard Books
A Division of Simon & Schuster, Inc.
1230 Avenue of the Americas
New York, NY 10020

First Howard Books hardcover edition April 2013

HOWARD and colophon are trademarks of Simon & Schuster, Inc.

For information about special discounts for bulk purchases, please contact Simon & Schuster Special Sales at 1-866-506-1949 or business@simonandschuster.com.

The Simon & Schuster Speakers Bureau can bring authors to your live event. For more information or to book an event, contact the Simon & Schuster Speakers Bureau at 1-866-248-3049 or visit our website at www.simonspeakers.com.

Designed by Renato Stanisic

Permissions appear on page 241.

Manufactured in the United States of America

10 9 8 7 6 5 4 3 2 1

Library of Congress Cataloging-in-Publication Data
Walker, Clay
Jesus was a country boy : life lessons on faith, fishing, and forgiveness / Clay Walker.
— 1st Howard Books hardcover ed.
p. cm.
1. Jesus Christ—Person and offices. 2. Walker, Clay, 1969– I. Title.
BT203.W35 2013
232.9'04—dc23
2012034311

ISBN 978-1-4516-8286-1
ISBN 978-1-4516-8287-8 (ebook)

To my dad, Ernest Clayton Walker Sr.

Contents

CONTENTS

CONTENTS

Chapter 9
Grace Amazing—He Gave It All for
the Sake of Love 209

JESUS WAS A
COUNTRY BOY

Introduction

Humble Beginnings

Walkin' down a dirt road with everything that he owned
He never met a stranger
Born in a barn, underneath the stars
His mama laid him in a manger
Swimmin' in the river, fishin' for his dinner,
Livin' with the sinners like me
Makes me think that Jesus was a country boy
—FROM "JESUS WAS A COUNTRY BOY"

'll never forget the first time I visited a big-city church. I guess it's what we'd call a mega-church now, over a thousand people in a big old building that looked like a cross between a stained-glass cathedral and an industrial warehouse. Barely twenty at the time, I had agreed to visit at the request of my then girlfriend, who wanted to show me off to her grandparents. They were pillars of the church and showed up every time the doors opened. I was smart enough to know that if the relationship was going anywhere, I'd need Grandma and Grandpa's approval.

You bet I was nervous. Growing up in the country, I was used to the little brick chapel down the road just across from the clapboard church with the steeple on top. While we always tried to wear our Sunday best, in Texas where I grew up this might mean your cleanest pair of blue jeans and the shirt your mama ironed that morning. So when I visited this big-city church for the first time, I wore the newest pair of jeans I owned and ironed my shirt myself (which means it still had quite a few wrinkles).

My girlfriend looked as beautiful as a spring buttercup in her yellow dress, and she told me that I cleaned up pretty nice, too. Going through the massive church doors into the cool, quiet sanctuary, I felt more like I was in the lobby of the Ritz-Carlton than in church. Plush carpet padded my boots, along with everyone else's, and insulated the noise of people talking. Dark green plants in huge ceramic urns guarded the pulpit, which looked more like a stage than a pulpit. Men in dark suits with white shirts and striped ties escorted ladies in high-necked dresses and flowing skirts.

"Baby, you didn't tell me we were going to a funeral!" I whispered and laughed.

She didn't seem to enjoy my joke and instead gave me the evil eye and whispered that I better stay on my best behavior. It was downhill from there. As we sat down on the polished mahogany pew with her grandparents, I noticed that I was the only one in jeans. As a robed choir marched in to the strains of a massive pipe organ, I realized that the people around us were looking at me. You know, looking at me as if I was some homeless man who'd wandered in off the street. The kind you're afraid might throw up on the carpet or steal money out of the collection plate. Those kinds of looks. Needless to say, I didn't feel welcome.

The music was just as proper and tight-lipped. It's hard to drain the soul out of good old-fashioned Baptist hymns, but this congregation sure tried. The pastor was equally as perfect, polished, and painful. His three-piece pinstripe suit fit him like a glove, and I recognize now that it had probably been hand-tailored by some Italian designer. He spoke in a strong, congenial voice that reminded me of a politician making a stump speech.

I'm sure he was a good man and probably knew more

about theology than I ever will, but . . . he didn't seem acquainted with the God I knew. The God who peeks out from the horizon each morning through the golden eyes of the sun. The God who smiles when I go fishing with my daddy and catch a bigger catfish than he does. The God who asks us to love our neighbor as we love ourselves, even if that neighbor is dressed in jeans instead of a suit.

Instead, the good reverend exposited the Bible, reminded us of his degrees and expertise as a trained seminarian, regretted how sinful people were outside the Church, and conducted an offering at the beginning *and* at the end of the service. My girlfriend seemed a little uncomfortable, but I could tell she wasn't going crazy on the inside the way I was. Like her grandparents, she smiled vaguely and nodded as if this were their favorite place to be on a Sunday morning.

You probably won't be surprised to hear that I never went back. Or that my girlfriend and I broke up a couple weeks later. Apparently, this country boy wasn't good enough for the fine folks at the First Big Downtown Church. And you know what? That was fine by me because I realized then that faith isn't about how you dress or how much theology you understand or where you sit on a Sunday morning. No, real faith—the kind that's connected to the love of God as our heavenly Daddy—starts with what's inside. And inside, I'm as country as it gets.

Real Country

The songs I sing come from this same place. From knowing the soft crush of spring grass beneath my bare feet. From knowing the steady rhythm of a woodpecker playing drums on a cottonwood tree. And the way a barn smells with its rich scent of mud, hay, and manure. The way a sliver of moon dangles in the darkness like a silver fishhook. The taste of corn bread and fried chicken washed down with sweet tea at my grandmother's table.

When I say I'm as country as it gets, I'm not kidding. I grew up living in a little white two-bedroom house that my grandparents bought for $35 during the Great Depression on a parcel of land off Erie Street about three miles outside of Beaumont, Texas. It had hardwood floors worn smooth by bare feet, a woodburning stove, and no air-conditioning other than a sultry breeze through an open window. In fact, I was twenty years old before I lived in a place that had AC!

We were surrounded by woods and rice fields, and there were no streetlights except for the stars glittering above the trees. It was out-in-the-country quiet with only the sound of the wind, a few crickets, maybe an old owl or whippoorwill, and the occasional coyote howling from the woods. Our nearest neighbors were miles away, and we were even farther from the local post office, grocery store, and gas station.

As a boy I loved wandering the rice fields and levees, the swampland and creeks, all around our house. With chickens scattering and dogs chasing me, I'd retreat to the woods to find a shady spot beneath the big oaks and evergreens, the sycamore and hickory trees. The branches overhead would stitch the dappled sunlight with patches of blue sky into a giant quilt rustling in the wind.

I'm proud of the way I grew up hard and have so many great memories I wouldn't trade for anything in this world. But growing up in the country the way I did was never easy. We kept a vegetable garden not as a hobby but as a necessity. The hogs we raised were not to show with the 4-H Club at the county fair but to butcher and freeze for the long winter ahead. And hunting was not a sport with camo suits, orange vests, expensive rifles, and tree stands. No, hunting was about putting meat on the table—duck, rabbit, squirrel, deer, even raccoons!

I was—and still am—an unabashed, unglorified country boy. I knew we were poor, but we never went hungry and always had a roof over our head. My siblings and I had to make our own fun, use our imagination, and sing along to George Strait and Reba McEntire on the radio in our daddy's truck. As hard as it was at times, I still loved every minute of it and appreciate the way it shaped me into the man I am today.

Growing up country, *real* country, I learned about God firsthand. Not just from the beauty of his creation all around me, but from seeing my sweet mother plead the blood of Jesus as she prayed for the safety of her children. I learned about God from how our neighbors treated us—lending us a mule to help plow the garden or bringing over a basket of fresh string beans. I learned about him from the way my family loved me and showed me how to love other people, no matter how different they might be from us. I learned about him from my Catholic grandmother, who read the Bible with me every night. And I learned about him from an Assembly of God preacher, Rev. David Hunter, who led me to give my heart to Jesus when I was fifteen years old. Cathocostal! I believe Jesus is not going to check your denomination card when you enter the gate. It's on the honor system . . . do you believe John 3:16?

I'm sickened by some of the biases that I've seen in some of the denominations. I've seen preachers spend fifteen to twenty minutes preaching against other denominations . . . is there really time for that? I've seen one spend time prohibiting other denominations from partaking communion with them. Really? Is this what it's come to? Would Christ approve of these shepherds and the way they're attending his flock? Is this really what Jesus would do?

I don't think so. These people who claim to be Bible

scholars, but treat others with disdain, don't know anything. You have to believe and be better than these Pharisees.

What Money Can't Buy

It's just all the more reason that I'm troubled at the way so many people get God confused with religion these days. Whether it's an experience like the one I had at my old girlfriend's church or the impression I get when I channel surf and find a slick TV preacher promising health and wealth for a regular monthly "contribution," I have to wonder. In fact, it was watching a televangelist strut and perform in his Armani suit, all the while begging for "seed money" for "God's kingdom," that inspired me to write the song "Jesus Was a Country Boy."

Maybe you've heard it (it's one of my favorites, so I hope you have!). The point I wanted to make in the song is that what (and who) we often see representing God in the world around us doesn't represent him accurately. As I write in the song, "'Cause it ain't who you are, it's who you know." The truth, as I see it at least, is that when God decided to send His Son down to live with us on Earth, he didn't set him up with a cable channel and a congregation of ten thousand people in fancy suits and dresses.

No, Jesus grew up just as country as I did, if not more so. While the Jewish people at the time expected the Messiah to be born in a palace surrounded by royalty, the Son of God came to us as a baby in a manger surrounded by shepherds and their smelly sheep. Jesus's earthly daddy was a carpenter, and Jesus took up the same trade until it was time to go public with his ministry. And what did he do when it was time to go public? A press conference? A big fund-raiser with water-into-wine and hors d'oeuvres made from loaves and fishes? A dedication for the new mega-synagogue in town?

I'm not trying to be irreverent here, only to support my point. No, what Jesus did was seek out his opening act, a wild-haired dude named John the Baptist, who had been paving the way for the Savior for some time. Jesus asked John to baptize him, and while the desert warrior in his camel-hair suit resisted at first ("You want *me* to baptize *you*?"), he finally agreed and dunked Jesus into the Jordan River. As the Son of God came up from the water gasping for air, the sky opened above him and a dove descended, not stopping until God's Spirit nested in his heart. "This is my beloved son in whom I am well pleased," boomed the Father with the joyful pride of any daddy watching his children.

Now, what's interesting to me is that Jesus hasn't done, well . . . anything yet! He hasn't performed any miracles or healed anyone or shared the Lord's Prayer or preached the Sermon on the Mount. Basically, he just showed up and got baptized. And God beamed and blessed him. My point is that Jesus didn't have to perform or work hard to earn his father's love. He just had to receive it.

From then on, he's in the public spotlight one way or another. While he may be a small-town boy (born in Bethlehem, raised in Nazareth), Jesus never forgets his humble beginnings when he heads to the big city of Jerusalem. He recruits guys—mostly fishermen and local joes—for his ministry team down at the docks, not from the Holy Rollers of his day, the Pharisees and Sadducees. He picks guys like Peter, an uneducated, rough-around-the-edges type who would become the rock upon which Christ built the Church.

They take each day as it comes, eating with tax collectors and talking to shady ladies, spending time with anyone who expresses an interest in knowing the truth. Whether a rich young ruler or a poor widow, a soldier with a sick daughter or a short guy in a sycamore tree, Jesus never met a stranger. He loved everyone he encountered and saw them for who they really were. He didn't try to impress them or sell them anything. He didn't ask for their money or monthly contributions. He asked only for their hearts. No games.

If Jesus were alive today, I think he'd be out doing the same kinds of things he did over two thousand years ago—meeting people where they are, healing those with aching backs and broken hearts, eating fish around a campfire on the beach, sharing stories about what matters most. Maybe I'm wrong, but I don't think he'd be leading a mega-church or hosting a daily talk show or running for political office. There's nothing wrong with any of those endeavors, and we need godly people in these positions. But if our picture of God comes only from those places, then we lose sight of what faith—and love and hope and forgiveness—are all about.

No doubt I'm biased in thinking people who grew up country are more authentic than folks who are caught up in the rat race of more, bigger, better. But what I've found is that country doesn't refer to where you grew up as much as where your heart grows down, where it takes root. Country is a state of mind. I believe what ultimately defines being country is simple: a loving heart, a helping hand, an open mind, poor in spirit. Like the person coming through the soup line at the shelter looking for a hot meal, we need to approach God with humility, hunger, and hope. When I see a beggar on the street, I'm reminded of how I want to approach God, not worthy or deserving but needy and wanting, asking him for what only he can give me.

Whether you're from Louisiana or Los Angeles, Tallahassee or Toronto, Nashville or Newark, if you're reading this right now, chances are good that you're country at heart.

If we want to grow in our faith, I don't think we have to go to church to find God. Too often, people treat church as the playground where they hide from the battlefield of life. Well, recess is over, and it's time to put our beliefs into practice in the real world. If we want to love our spouses more and show our children what it means to be an honest man or an honest woman, then we have only to come back to our roots. Practicing values like courage and respect, honor and decency. Enjoying a high school football game on a Friday night. Thanking our veterans when we have the opportunity. Loving people where they are. Keeping our word no matter what.

Whether we call it being country or being Christian, this way of life doesn't rely on religion to know God. It relies on folks like you and me who want to live more, love more, and laugh more. In fact, if we look to Jesus as our example, if we consider that he himself understood what it means to be genuine, real-deal country, then we can learn best from his example.

If we really want to be closer to God, more passionately alive to all the blessings around us, and more in love with the life we've been given, then we only have to look to Jesus.

I'm no theologian and I'm not a preacher, but I do know how much God loves me and I continue to live for him each day. If you'll allow me the privilege, I'd like to share some thoughts with you in the pages that follow on what I've learned by returning to Jesus—not big churches or TV preachers—to define my faith.

My hope is that you'll find some wisdom for living, some inspiration for loving, and some stories that will make you smile. I believe Jesus was a country boy, and his earthy, honest faith and real, heartfelt love changed the course of time and history. If we keep our country roots, then our faith will grow and our lives will be richer in the things that money can't buy.

Jesus Knew How to LIVE

★

CHAPTER 1

Never Met a Stranger—He Knew How to Treat People

Just the way I'm helping you
If you really want to pay me back,
Here's what you do
Don't let the chain of love end with you
—FROM "THE CHAIN OF LOVE"

Celebrity status is pretty easy to come by in our world today. Reality shows, the Internet, YouTube, and Facebook make it possible for anyone to grab their fifteen minutes in the public spotlight. If you're talented enough, clever enough, funny enough, or persistent enough, chances are good that you can get thousands of people to notice you. What they think of you, however, may be another thing altogether.

Sure, there's the face we give to the world, but we've all learned that what you see is not necessary what's really inside a person. Good friends of mine, the kind who've known me all my life, tell me that they often get asked, "What's Clay *really* like?" My friends tell me that they take great pleasure in being able to tell the truth. Without blowing my own horn, I'm proud that they can tell people that with Clay Walker, what you see is what you get. I'm not trying to be one person onstage or in an interview or on TV and then someone else behind the scenes when I'm with my family and friends.

And it's not always easy being true to yourself, especially in a culture that judges you by what you wear, what you drive, who you know, and where you live. We place so much importance on the roles we play and the toys we can afford that we forget about what it means to be a good person. The kind of man or woman who treats you the same way whether you're dressed up or dressed down, in the checkout line at the 7-Eleven or in the receiving line at the governor's mansion.

Our jobs can complicate the way others see us and treat us, and the way we respond to them. Granted, the music industry is a little bit crazier than most normal businesses. My manager tells me it's because the artists and songwriters are all a little bit crazy—like me! I take that as a compliment, and I realize that while the music business is unique in many ways, there's one fundamental way that it's the same as any other: the way you treat people.

Building Noah's Ark

Recently, I ordered a big wooden boat for my son's birthday. It was going to be a cross between a giant rowboat and a playhouse and was going to look like Noah's Ark. Yep, I know what you're thinking—it sounds like something guaranteed to spoil a three-year-old, and you're probably right. But if you'd seen the way his eyes lit up when we were reading the Bible story about Noah and all the animals and the flood, and then heard the tone of his voice when he asked if maybe we should build an ark and put it on the big old bass pond on our farm, you wouldn't have been able to resist him, either!

So I decided to get this miniature ark for him for his birthday and surprise him. It had to be custom-built, and some friends of mine told me just where to go for it. A few weeks later someone from the boat shop called and told me it was ready. Almost as excited as my son would be to see the finished ark, I left right away to go see it before the shop closed. I'd been working in the barn most of the day but didn't want to take the time to get cleaned up.

Now I knew I looked a little grubby in my old sweatpants, T-shirt, and ball cap, and I probably smelled a little like the barn, too, but didn't think twice about stopping. The boat place reminded me of the woodshop at my old high school, a giant warehouse with lots of tools, ramps, hitches, and a few pulleys hanging from the rafters. The guys there wouldn't mind.

So I stopped at the boat shop, talked to the owner, and paid him; he handed me off to one of his crew to show me Noah's Ark. We were moving fast, and the owner didn't introduce me, and I didn't think of it at the time—I just wanted to see the ark! So my guide to the ark—I'll call him Troy—took me to a corner of the warehouse and pointed out a giant rowboat that would've made Noah proud.

Although I was definitely preoccupied with my new ark, I couldn't miss noticing that my guy Troy had an attitude. Now I'm used to being recognized from time to time, and it's no big deal. I usually enjoy connecting with another fan of country music, and if they happen to like mine, then I'm even happier. But with my new friend Troy, it was clear that he didn't know me from Adam.

Maybe it was the curt way he nodded and grunted, or the way he refused to return my attempt at small talk. Maybe it was the way he looked at my dirty clothes and muddy boots and worn ball cap, the kind of look I hadn't seen since visiting that big-city downtown church with my old girlfriend. The kind of look that made me feel like a homeless person lying in an alleyway.

Needless to say, Troy didn't share my giddy joy as I surveyed the details of the ark. He just stood there like a statue with his arms crossed, impatiently waiting on me to hurry up and leave so he could get back to waiting on the real customers. I asked if he would be on the delivery truck that would be bringing it out to our farm the next day. He said he would, so I gave him directions, thanked him, and headed on my way.

I didn't think any more about my buddy Troy or the boat until the next day when I was out at the farm waiting on the truck and trailer that would bring Noah's Ark. I had just come from a business meeting in town and looked a little nicer and a lot cleaner. Nothing fancy, but my dark jeans, western shirt, and polished boots painted a different image than my farmhand duds from the day before. That, along with my name on the mailbox, and probably the size of the place, made it clear that I was a very lucky man, a guy named Clay Walker.

When Troy saw me, he immediately came over, shook my hand, and tried to call me "Mr. Walker" before I corrected him. I tried to be friendly, but my mind really was on how to get the ark down to the pond without getting the trailer stuck in the mud. Troy's mind, however, was on telling me that he used to be a musician for a country music superstar—a name you'd recognize—a few years back. He'd toured with this person for years before "things changed," and he'd ended up in his present job. He didn't come right out and ask me for a job, but he sure got mighty close. The sunrise shift of his dark attitude couldn't have been more glaring.

The Golden Yardstick

I tell you this story not to pass any judgment on Troy and certainly not to make myself look any better. But the dramatic shift in how he treated me once he knew who I was reminded me of what one of my mentors in the music industry once told me. It was after a show in a little honky-tonk outside of Dallas, and I had opened for this older, well-established performer. I was feeling grumpy after the show because a lot of little things had gone wrong—the owner not following through on details he'd told me would be handled. My older, wiser friend knew I wanted to lash out and agreed that I probably had every right to. But he said something I'll never forget.

"Clay," he said, "you'll discover in this business there's two reasons people will remember you. One's the quality of the music you make, and you make some damn fine music. The second is how you treat 'em. Not just the decision makers, but the waitresses, the roadies, the gophers, and the crew. So far, you're easy to get along with and know that you're no better than anyone else. Don't ever change."

His words meant the world to me. I'm no saint: I lose my patience when I'm driving or I get mad when someone cuts in line just like anyone else. But I try to remember how I want to be treated and what it means to walk a mile in another man's shoes. This is the Golden Rule, or as my grandmother used to call it, "the golden yardstick." In fact, I remember an incident one time when she broke that yardstick across my twelve-year-old backside for not following the Golden Rule!

Thanks to her loving correction, wise words from my mentors, and the hard lessons of life, I learned to value the Golden Rule as my own. I learned that even when you try your best you can't always control your reputation, those perceptions and expressed opinions of others toward you. But I also know that character, who you really are inside, is something that God always sees.

So I always try to treat people the way that Jesus would treat them. When asked, he said, "So in everything, do to others what you would have them do to you, for this sums up the Law and the Prophets" (Matthew 7:12). Rich or poor, short or tall, man or woman, old or young, insider or outsider, Jesus loved them all. In both word and deed, he walked what he talked.

Short Stuff

While Jesus consistently treated all people with compassion and respect, there's one of his encounters that especially stands out for me. It involves a short weasel of a man with a funny-sounding name. Since my kids have a hard time saying "Zacchaeus" (a name I'm told means "clean and pure"—funny, considering he was a crooked tax collector!), when we read this story at bedtime, I just call him Short Stuff.

The story goes that Jesus was on his way into the town of Jericho, and large crowds had gathered because they'd heard about this man who could teach the Scriptures better than any rabbi and who could heal the sick better than any doctor. One person in particular, a tax collector who'd gotten rich by taking his own cut, was curious and wanted to see for himself what all the fuss was about. Only problem was that Short Stuff couldn't see above the crowd. At this point I remind my kids of how they felt at the Christmas parade *before* their mom and I put them on our shoulders.

Since Zacchaeus couldn't sit on someone's shoulders, he did the next best thing and found a sycamore tree to climb. Up on an extended branch, he could perch and spy on everyone who passed by, including Jesus. Funny thing, though, was that Jesus veered off the road and came right over to where Short Stuff was hiding. It strikes me that even when we try to hide from God, he knows where to find us and invites us to receive the gift of his love. Which is exactly what Jesus offered our buddy Z:

When Jesus reached the spot, he looked up and said to him, "Zacchaeus, come down immediately. I must stay at your house today." So he came down at once and welcomed him gladly.

All the people saw this and began to mutter, "He has gone to be the guest of a sinner."

But Zacchaeus stood up and said to the Lord,

*"Look, Lord! Here and now I give half of my posses-
sions to the poor, and if I have cheated anybody out of
anything, I will pay back four times the amount."*

*Jesus said to him, "Today salvation has come to
this house, because this man, too, is a son of Abraham.
For the Son of Man came to seek and to save the lost."*
(Luke 19:5–10)

I always imagined that Jesus might've paused for a couple
seconds in between "Zacchaeus, come down here!" and "I'm
hangin' at your house today!" And in those few seconds, poor
Short Stuff must've thought, Busted! If this Jesus knows I'm
up in this tree and he knows my name, then he must know
who I am and the kind of man I am. In fact, from the little
information we're told, it would've been justifiable and logical if Jesus had called him on the grass carpet.

But the Savior must've smiled then and made it clear
that he wasn't there to condemn Zacchaeus but to care for
him. Yes, Jesus knew who he was, all right. He knew that
this little man was more than just a callous tax collector and
thief. He knew that there was a desire for more, a desire to
change, a longing to be loved and not judged inside Zacchaeus's heart.

Sure enough, our tree hugger couldn't believe his good fortune! Jesus—the one everybody's talking about and wants a piece of—this Jesus wants to come to his house! The crowd, however, had a much different response. Instead of believing that Short Stuff could be anything more than who they've labeled him as, they decided that Jesus must not be so special after all. If he's willing "to be the guest of a sinner," then Jesus must be just as crooked, conniving, and low-class as the tax collector.

Jesus wasn't surprised, nor did he seem to care. Because what he cared about—rescuing the heart of the man who longed for a way out of the tangled mess of a life he'd created—changes Zacchaeus's life forever. Our buddy Short Stuff was so overwhelmed that he was like Ebenezer Scrooge on Christmas morning! On the spot he proclaimed that he was giving away half of his money to the poor, and on top of that, he was going to refund four times the amount he'd stolen from others.

As we consider Jesus's concluding words here, his message couldn't be clearer. He says, "Today salvation has come to this man's house, because he, too, is a son of Abraham." I take this to mean that those people whom we tend to judge and shun and push aside because they're different aren't so different after all. Basically, by calling Zacchaeus a "son of

Abraham," Jesus was saying that not only is this tax collector a Jew just like the rest of you, but that he is a holy man, a royal descendant of the patriarch of the Jewish nation and its faith in the one true God. This was usually a phrase reserved for the high priests and religious leaders, not for an average joe, especially not one as crooked and despicable as Shorty. Jesus wraps up his point by saying that the reason he was there was to seek and save the lost—even people that everyone else would give up on, people like Zacchaeus.

People like you and me.

Driving Me Crazy

I know what it's like to be looked down upon like the townspeople looked down upon Zacchaeus. Not literally, since I reckon I'm a bit taller than he was, but growing up as poor as I did, I sure knew the feeling of having others think they're better than me. Most of the cars I drove as a teenager were at least ten to twenty years old, covered in mud from the dirt roads we lived near, and missing a headlight, hubcap, or hardtop. I don't need to tell you how the other kids at my high school regarded me or how many jokes they cracked at my expense. Many of them had families in the oil and gas business and made lots of money, which meant they drove Mustangs, Corvettes, and new F-150s. When I pulled up in my old, mud-splattered Pontiac rust bucket, the contrast couldn't have been any greater.

At my present stage of life, I've gone from being the poorest of the poor to being at the other end of the spectrum. I've worked hard and done my best, and God has blessed me beyond anything I could've ever imagined back in Beaumont. Now I enjoy having more than one vehicle to drive, and they're usually paid for in cash and driven off the lot brand-new.

Funny thing, though, is that I'm still being judged. A few years back, I was going to play golf at a local country club near my home in Texas. It was a nice club, but not a fancy, snobby-type place—more like a great sports facility with a golf course. So I happened to be driving a sleek, black Jaguar XJ that I had at that time when I pulled up at the course to play a round. As I looked around for the friends I was meeting for the game, our caddy unloaded my clubs. While he stood waiting for us, an older gentleman came up next to him, probably waiting for his own clubs to be unloaded. I was only a few feet from them, and I couldn't believe what I overheard.

"Nice car, that Jag there," said the older man. "Shame it ain't paid for."

The caddy, a young college-age guy, raised his eyebrows in surprise as the man continued sharing his opinion.

"Yep, that young fellow I saw getting out of that car is in way over his head. There's no way he could be driving a Jaguar as young as he is and not be overextended. Some people just can't live within their means."

Well, as you can imagine, this little conversation had my attention by now! Part of me was amused at this gentleman's assessment based on his misperception and personal prejudices. The other part of me was madder than a hornet's nest. All of a sudden the sting of shame I'd once felt in my high school parking lot came rushing back to me. Once again, I was being judged and looked down on based on the car I drove! I'd gone from a beat-up Pontiac to a shiny new Jag, but the opinions and judgments of others were the same. I couldn't win!

Lost in my thoughts, I came back to their conversation in time to hear the young caddy say, "Sir, I don't know if you recognized the driver of that car or not, but he's Clay Walker. The country music singer."

Now it was the older man's turn to raise his eyebrows and look surprised.

"I think it's a safe bet that the car is paid for," the caddy said, and smiled.

About that time, my friends arrived, and we headed for

the course. I didn't tell our caddy that I'd heard the conversation, but I made sure that he got an extra big tip that day for watching my back! I like to think that I would have stood up for him if he'd driven up in an old, beat-up Pontiac and I had been his caddy.

Chain of Love

Jesus made it clear that how we treat other people says a lot about who we are, how we see ourselves, and how we view God. It's so easy to get caught up in our world's way of looking at life that we end up getting away from our country roots and losing sight of who we are and what we believe. Which is why we have to be reminded that every encounter we have with another human being matters. The young cashier in the grocery store, the gray-haired greeter at Walmart, your son's piano teacher, or your daughter's soccer coach . . . they all matter. While you don't have to have a deep, meaningful conversation with every person you see today, you never know when a simple act of kindness might have a huge ripple effect.

This is the idea behind a song I recorded called "The Chain of Love," which I cowrote with Rory Lee Feek. It tells the story of a rich lady from St. Louis driving along in her Mercedes when she has a flat tire. Stranded on the side of the highway in the snow, hundreds of cars pass her by without stopping. Finally, a beat-up Pontiac pulls up and a big man gets out and lumbers over to her. She's a little scared at first until he introduces himself as Joe and reassures her that he's there to help.

Joe fixes her tire and has her car ready to hit the road again. When the lady asks him what she owes him, Joe tells her that he's been in her place before and knows what it's like to need a helping hand. So he asks her to just "pay it forward" by helping out someone else down the line, thereby adding another link in the "chain of love."

The lady thanked him and went on her way then stopped a few miles later to eat lunch at a small café. The food tasted so good and the hot coffee warmed her up after all that time waiting with the flat tire in the cold. Her waitress was a pretty young woman who seemed genuinely kind and gave her such speedy service despite the fact that she was clearly about to have a baby in a matter of weeks, if not days.

With the kindness from her tire-changing hero fresh in her mind, the lady left a hundred-dollar bill beneath her check for $5.37, along with a note asking the young mother-to-be to keep the chain of love alive. The story concludes when the waitress goes home that night, dead tired on her feet and still thinking about the money and the lady's note. Crawling under the covers beneath her hardworking husband who was already fast asleep, she whispers, "Everything's gonna be alright. I love you, Joe."

I had fun sharing that story in the form of a song, and a lot of people have told me how much it's made them stop and think about the little things each day. How sometimes even smiling at someone can make their day, or having a friend call for no reason other than that they're thinking about them, or having a customer representative do a great job in solving a problem. Between people, the little things matter each day. Fixing a flat tire. Leaving a giant tip for someone in need. Connecting with a friend who spots you in a crowd. Getting a cool drink on a sweltering day.

Jesus knew how to treat other people, and he continues to give us a model that's as relevant now as it was thousands of years ago. Like he did with Zacchaeus, his parents and disciples, and so many others, he looked beyond surface appearances and discerned human hearts. He knew that we can fool people—for better and for worse—by the way we look and the role we fill. He knew that sometimes we resign ourselves to being who other people tell us we are—a crook, a gold digger, a liar, a thief—even though that's not who we really are or want to be.

I like to think that Jesus continues to call each one of us

down from the trees where we try to hide from him and remind us what it means to be loved and forgiven. Just like the Samaritan woman at the well, I believe he continues to offer each of us a spring-cold drink of water that quenches us way down deep beyond the cool trickle in our throats.

And I believe we have the same privilege of being Jesus to those around us and offering them the same life-giving encounters. While we don't owe God anything for the gift of life he brings to us, if you've received his many blessings, then you know we owe him everything. With this in mind, I truly believe these words are much more his than mine: "If you really want to pay me back, / Here's what you do / Don't let the chain of love end with you."

CHAPTER 2

Rebel with a Cause—He Wasn't Afraid of a Fight

I was raised knowin' right from wrong
Baptized under that old rugged cross
I try to be a good man, I always give it my best
But truth be told some days I wanna go to the
wild, wild west
I know where to draw the line
But there's just something 'bout that other side
I got angels on my left, and demons on my right
It's a never-ending battle, it's a constant fight

—FROM "JESSE JAMES"

When my music career started, I'd play in just about any place that would have me. Most times it was just my guitar and me, sometimes with a house band or handful of friends, but usually just me. Which meant I had to make sure that I knew where I was going, how to get there, and what time I could set up and do a sound check before going on. A lot of these places were bars, of course, and most of the time they provided small but lively audiences. Sometimes, though, things got a little rowdy and ended up turning into a barroom brawl.

While I witnessed a number of them, I actually once started one of my own. I was playing in a little bar in Beaumont, Texas, and spotted the guy who had stolen my PA equipment a few weeks earlier. After I finished my set, I went and tried to talk to him like a gentleman and told him that he needed to return my gear right away or face the consequences. He said, "Not gonna happen," and turned his back on me and resumed his conversation.

As calmly as I could, I went to the pay phone in the back and called my dad. "Daddy, it's Clay. Listen, I may need you to bail me out of jail later tonight. I just thought I'd call and give you a heads-up."

"Why's that?" he asked.

I filled him in on the situation and told him I was about to get in a fight to get my PA gear back.

"Well, if you're going to get in a fight," he said, "I've only got one piece of advice for you, son. *Win!*" And we both started laughing.

I don't remember much more after that phone call, but I reckon both the other fellow and I got some punches in. And for the record, I got the last one in and did indeed get my stolen gear from the back of his truck. Being older and wiser now (well, at least sometimes), I'm sure there were other ways I could've handled the situation more diplomatically. But you know what? Maybe not. Sometimes you have to be willing to fight for what's right.

Don't Mess with Jesus

As unlikely as it may seem, my views on when and what to fight for have been shaped the most by another country boy who wasn't afraid to stand up for what's right: Jesus Christ. Now, maybe you're like I used to be and view Jesus as this gentle, kind, and compassionate young man with long, flowing hair, a nice tan, and a toothpaste-commercial-white smile. A peacemaker. A healer. A teacher. A guy who just wanted everyone to love God and love one another, right?

Wrong.

While Jesus is certainly a peacemaker, healer, and teacher, if you read about him in the Gospels, it's clear that he wasn't one to tiptoe on eggshells or just telling people what they wanted to hear. The dude knew how to stir people up and didn't care whom he offended with the truth of God. He was more rebel than rabbi, more warrior than weakling, and more confronter than compromiser. Jesus was a fighter, and he knew which battles to pick and which ones to ignore. He was a country boy who minded his manners but also didn't mind standing up for what was right. Where I'm from we have a saying, "Don't mess with Texas." But I think we can also add "Don't mess with Jesus."

Don't believe me? Then let's consider a few examples of Jesus in action. One of my favorite stories about him has always been when he drives the money changers from the temple. Maybe I love it because it shows us that even the Son of God gets angry and takes action sometimes. He's not just the "baby in the manger" or the "gentle shepherd" watching over his flock and performing miracles. The scene in the temple with the money changers shows us he's a take-no-prisoners kind of man's man who doesn't suffer fools. See for yourself:

When it was almost time for the Jewish Passover, Jesus went up to Jerusalem. In the temple courts he found people selling cattle, sheep and doves, and others sitting at tables exchanging money. So he made a whip out of cords, and drove all from the temple courts, both sheep and cattle; he scattered the coins of the money changers and overturned their tables. To those who sold doves he said, "Get these out of here! Stop turning my Father's house into a market!" (John 2:13–16)

Maybe like me when I first read this passage, you're thinking, Isn't he overreacting? What's the big deal? Weren't they supposed to sacrifice animals in the temple? While the Jewish people in Jesus's day did sacrifice animals in atonement for their sins, it's clear that the scene Jesus encountered took things way too far. The emphasis was no longer on the sacrifice being made to purify themselves and restore their relationship with God. Instead it looked more like the stock pen at a rodeo roundup!

Or think of it this way. One of the things I love about going to a flea market is the variety of things you'll find there: vintage quilts, homemade candy, old metal tools, used furniture, eight-track tapes, antique glassware, new white tube socks. There's always a diversity of people there as well, some looking for bargains or *Antiques Roadshow*–type treasures and others intent on selling the junk they've collected over the years. At really large flea markets, there's almost a carnival-type atmosphere, with concession stands and a petting zoo for little kids thrown in.

Now imagine this kind of flea-market frenzy taking place in the back of the sanctuary inside your local church, and you'll have some idea what Jesus encountered when he went into the temple. This area that should have been a sacred, reverent place looked more like a street fair! And Jesus wasted no time in expressing his opinion of the situation. He didn't just say "Get out of here!" He grabbed some cords and fashioned a whip.

Just Whip It

While it's tempting to view his reaction as rash and impulsive, we need to keep two things in mind. First, we're told, "For we do not have a high priest who is unable to empathize with our weaknesses, but we have one who has been tempted in every way, just as we are—yet he did not sin" (Hebrews 4:15). So even though he's madder than a bull seeing red, Jesus never crossed the line into losing control and giving in to sin. Basically, this raises the point that there are two kinds of anger discussed in the Bible, righteous anger—which is what Jesus felt and acted on here—and unrighteous anger, which is usually what you and I experience in a traffic jam.

The second thing is that he took the time and "made

a whip out of cords," which he used to drive out every-thing and everyone—sheep, cattle, goats, and presumably their owners—from the temple courts. Now I don't know if you've ever tried to make your own whip out of strips of leather or frayed pieces of rope, but it's not something you do in a matter of seconds. It used to take a whole afternoon just to make a leather bracelet at 4-H camp—making a whip would've taken me all day!

So at the very least, Jesus took a few minutes to put to-gether a practical tool for accomplishing his objective. A whip is not something that you just wave in front of people—it gets them moving! He wasn't just waving a broom and shoo-ing them out of the temple the way my grandmother used to chase a cat out of the house. He meant business! When we think of someone using a whip as a kind of weapon, we usu-ally think of Indiana Jones or Zorro, but I think we should add Jesus to the list.

Like I said, this kind of Jesus might go against the meek-and-mild version that, like me, you may have grown up seeing in artists' renderings in Sunday school. You know, the ones where he's sadly smiling, looking at sheep or children in the distance, a gentle breeze blowing through his long rock-star-style hair. No, the picture we have of Jesus chas-ing the money changers out of the temple is a fierce warrior, a man who knows what's right and isn't afraid to fight for it. He's a guy you would not want to meet in a dark alley behind the temple—especially not with that whip!

Not-So-Holy Rollers

The money changers in the temple weren't the only ones with whom Jesus had a problem. He also seems to go off on most of the religious leaders of his day, a group called the Pharisees. Now these guys were supposed to be the ones leading the charge for God, inspiring others to love God, and serving those in need. Except the Pharisees were all about themselves and feeling smug about how special they were. To be blunt, they thought they were better than everyone else, thought they were the only ones with a direct line to God.

They actually said things like, "Lord, thank you that I'm not like those nasty old sinners over there." And they would go out in the middle of a crowd on the street to talk about how wonderful, how generous, how holy, and how *humble* they were. If you've ever flipped channels and stumbled across a slick TV preacher drawing out his syllables in a thick southern (why are these guys almost always from the South?) accent and begging you for "seed money" so the

Lord can bless you for blessing him, then you know the type we're talking about here.

As you can imagine, Jesus scared the unholy snot out of these Pharisees because he saw right through them and refused to play their game. They were mighty intimidated by this rebel who seemed to know and serve a different God—a loving, gracious God. He hung out with fishermen and prostitutes, tax collectors and poor people. He healed people and fed people and talked about the love of God. Jesus upset the Pharisees' apple cart, and so they started trying to trick him into saying something they could use against him. They constantly tested and tempted him, badgering and heckling him like a drunk at a bad concert.

So what did Jesus do? He told them the truth, plain and simple:

"Woe to you, teachers of the law and Pharisees, you hypocrites! You clean the outside of the cup and dish, but inside they are full of greed and self-indulgence. Blind Pharisee! First clean the inside of the cup and dish, and then the outside also will be clean.

"Woe to you, teachers of the law and Pharisees, you hypocrites! You are like whitewashed tombs, which look

beautiful on the outside but on the inside are full of the
bones of the dead and everything unclean. In the same
way, on the outside you appear to people as righteous
but on the inside you are full of hypocrisy and wicked-
ness." (Matthew 23:25–28)

Say What You Need to Say

Wow—it doesn't get much clearer than that, does it? Jesus calls them hypocrites, dirty dishes, and whitewashed tombs (and actually he's just getting started!). There's no doubt how he felt about them, and since he was the Son of God, he wasn't just venting or sharing his feelings. He was telling it like it was!

He didn't have time for their little games and their hypocritical pretense of being Holy Rollers. He didn't want other people to assume that they knew what they were talking about when it comes to God. They taught about a God of the law who allowed them, the Pharisees and other religious leaders, to be the gatekeepers to his kingdom. They claimed to be the ones who could give everyone else God's official seal of approval.

Only problem, though, is that all of us—even pastors, preachers, and Sunday school teachers—are sinful and selfish and make mistakes every day. We all need God's love, mercy, and grace, and once we experience those, we need to share them with everybody around us. Not just the rich or the famous or the smart or the successful—everybody. Including the poor and the obscure and the ignorant and those who mess up a lot. Jesus made it clear the Pharisees didn't have the market cornered on God. No one does! To quote my daddy, "I ain't never met no perfect son of a b——!"

That's why Jesus came—so each of us could know God individually and personally, without having to go through any kind of middleman who likely has his own agenda. Please don't get me wrong. Not all pastors, ministers, and religious are self-righteous and hypocritical—thank goodness, they're not! We do need them in our world today, and I'm grateful for all the wonderful things they do to motivate, inspire, teach, and serve everyone they encounter. But what we see in Jesus's response to the Pharisees is that we do not need to accept anyone else's judgment of our relationship with God as fact. What's between us and God is, well . . . between us and God!

One of my primary motivations for writing this book is to remind people that Jesus was not a big-shot, uppity religious leader. No, he was a good old boy, a man of integrity with old-fashioned, country values. And one of those values, as we see here in his sharp words to the Pharisees, is that he's not afraid to call a spade a spade and to say what others might be afraid to say. He never backed down from a fight that needed to be fought.

At the same time, I think it's important for us to realize that he didn't go around trying to provoke a fight and stir up trouble all the time. No, Jesus stayed focused on who he was and what he was on Earth to do. He didn't allow his detractors and critics to make his choices for him, like a lifetime politician at election time. But he also knew when to blister them with the heat of the truth about themselves.

Sometimes we have to say hard things, even to those people we love and care about. Early in my career, as people began to recognize me in public and stop me on the street, I tried to be friendly and nice to everyone. I enjoy interacting with my fans and don't forget that they're the reason for my success. I love talking to other people who love music, especially country music, as much as I do.

However, I also learned that there have to be limits to my kindness, because some people are always going to try to push too far. People who think they know me as their best friend because they listen to my music and read interviews. People who want to stalk my family and me so they can dispel up the loneliness in their own lives. People who try to take advantage of my kindness and exploit my compassion. People like the audio-tech specialist who was working on one of my tour buses a few years ago.

The bus was tricked out with a pretty fancy computer system that could lower the blinds, adjust the temperature, control the audio, dim the lights, and do just about everything except fry a burger for you. After returning from a tour, we had several problems with the audio system, so my driver took it to be looked at by a specialist in Houston, where I was living at the time. After reviewing the system, the tech shop sent me a bid for the cost of the repairs. Now, it was a hefty price, but I knew for a rig like mine it was going to cost a little more. But then when I called the next day, identified myself as the owner of the bus, all of a sudden that already steep price tag *quadrupled*! I told the tech "thanks but no thanks" and took my business elsewhere. Sadly enough, he erased the programming of the entire system, adding even more repairs for the next shop. But that's okay—I'd rather pay more to someone who's consistent and the same with everyone than someone who jacks up his fee because he recognizes his customer as a celebrity.

We all have people in our lives who can act like Pharisees and unethical audio techs—and we can even find ourselves acting like them sometimes. But the message that Jesus gives us reminds us that we have to stand up to the hypocrites and the people who claim to be better than everyone else. We have to stand up for the poor and the broken and the homeless and the imprisoned and the widowed and the orphaned. We have to remember that we're no better than any other person. We are all God's children and saved by his grace, not by how many times we go to church, how much we give to the TV preacher's ministry, or whom we know on the board of directors.

Sometimes we have to call out the Pharisees in our lives and quit worrying what they, or anyone else, will think. Following Jesus does not mean trying to be nice to everyone you meet. And the truth is, no matter how much you try to please others, you're never going to please everyone. Nor are we supposed to! We certainly need to treat others with respect and compassion, but sometimes they leave us no choice but to confront them with the truth. Sometimes we have to say what we need to say and let the chips fall where they may.

Fight Club

So why did Jesus have such a big problem with the money changers and Pharisees? The main reason seems to be what he himself says, that they had turned his Father's house into a marketplace and had turned the practice of relating to God into nothing but a legal document with themselves as presiding judges. The money changers had taken a sacred place intended for worship and turned it into a common place focused on commerce. The Pharisees had taken a personal relationship with the Living God and tried to put it in a box—their box. Both groups had sold out in a major way!

I can't help but think that God still feels the same way about the choices we make. In our celebrity-saturated world today, so many people are intent on getting their fifteen minutes of fame and making as much money as possible. But so many people discover the truth the hard way: money and fame don't make you happy. Discovering your special purpose on this earth and using it as God leads you to serve others makes you happy. Maybe it's because we live in a capitalist, product-driven culture, but so often even people who discover their gift, their special purpose in life, end up aiming it toward the world's definition of success and not the Lord's.

Now you may be thinking, Well, that's easy for you to say, Mr. Clay Walker. You get to do what you love—making music and performing—and get paid for it! As I've said before, I'm one lucky son of a gun, and I won't deny that I do indeed get paid for doing what I love the most. But I have also worked hard and tried to follow the right path and not just the shortest route or the flashiest road. And for over a decade now, I've also had to fight a daily battle I never saw coming, a tug-of-war with my own body.

The biggest fight of my life started at an old basketball court near Calgary, Alberta. I was touring Canada and having the time of my life. Audiences were great, and the country itself was amazingly beautiful. The day before my basketball game, we'd been in Golden, British Columbia, and my band guys and I had gone snowmobiling. Someone took a picture of me that day, and the joy I was experiencing shows through in my ear-to-ear smile.

Life was going great for Clay Walker. I was twenty-six years old, and I had just experienced the joy of my first child being born and the excitement of having my fourth album released. My career as a country music artist was accelerating with more and more concerts and constant airplay on radio stations. So on this particular day, I was looking forward to getting a little exercise with some of the guys in my band in a friendly game of hoops. We were all intensely competitive and enjoyed the ongoing rivalry that came with testing one another's abilities on the court.

We had barely gotten started that cold March day when it became clear that I wasn't on my game that day. Trying to block a shot, I fell on the asphalt. To the other guys, it appeared that I was fouled and making a really valiant play. But I knew the real reason I had fallen. It was as if my leg had just gone numb, unable to support my weight, sort of that feeling you have when your foot's asleep and you try to walk on it. I shook it off and got to my feet and assumed I was just really tired from the tour and the previous day's snowmobiling.

But then as the game progressed, I lost the feeling in my right arm. Whenever I tried to make a shot, it was always woefully off target. I started joking about it, and my buddies began teasing me, saying I'd gone soft or assuming that I was hung over from too much fun the night before. I couldn't bring myself to tell them that I hadn't had a thing to drink the night before. Maybe I'd just pulled a muscle, right?

Over the course of that game, I tripped or fell at least another three or four times. And my vision had also started blurring and doubling whatever I saw. At first, I thought it was just sweat from my forehead dripping into my eyes, but even after wiping my face, I found things still looked fuzzy. There was a weird tingle on one side of my face as well. I knew something was wrong, but I didn't want any of my friends to see the extent of my concern. So I just tried to laugh it off and keep going. Maybe I was just tired from all the stress and the constant demands of my newly successful music career.

The next day, I felt better, but the numbness, blurred vision, and muscle spasms on the side of my face continued. When I picked up my guitar that morning, I couldn't even hold the pick in my hand and strum a few chords. I was afraid to hold my baby girl for fear I'd drop her. I knew I couldn't ignore this any longer and found myself scheduling a doctor's appointment right away. A few days later, I was told I had lesions on my brain from a chronic neurological disorder known as multiple sclerosis (MS), a disease that attacks the brain and spinal cord.

When I asked my doctor if I'd be able to continue playing guitar, he stared at me for a moment. "Mr. Walker," my doctor said grimly, "this is more serious. I'm afraid within four years you'll be in a wheelchair, unable to walk under your own power." I looked at him in wide-eyed disbelief. "And in eight years . . . well, I'm afraid you'll be dead." In what felt like just a matter of days, I'd gone from being on top of the world to being crushed by the weight of it.

Anger Management

Before I was diagnosed with MS, I wouldn't have called myself a hothead, but now, looking back, it's easy to see that I definitely had some anger-management issues. Maybe it came from being young and stupid, feeling invulnerable and impatient, but I would often fly off the handle at little things.

You know, the kinds of things that life throws at us every day. Someone cuts you off on the highway and then has the nerve to flip a rude gesture in your direction, as if you'd been the one driving recklessly. Back then, this kind of thing would've been a good reason to run 'em down and have a nice roadside chat.

Or someone treats you rudely for no good reason—a waitress, a salesclerk, a checker at the store—and you lash out at him or her and make it clear that you won't be pushed around. You retaliate with a smart-ass remark or a tongue-lashing to the manager. Not to mention the way my quick temper could set me off with friends or family. Not to mention a friendly (or not-so-friendly) bar fight on occasion.

Looking back, I like to think my fighting spirit came from growing up hard and having to scrap and scrape for everything that I owned. I had learned early in life that nothing came easy and that you had to look out for yourself if you ever wanted to get ahead. You had to remain on high alert at all times to prevent the next guy from taking advantage of you or ripping you off. Most people really couldn't be trusted, I thought, so I better be ready to fight at a moment's notice. It's how you learned to be a man in Texas.

Even if my environment did influence my hard stance against the world, it still didn't excuse it. And it wasn't that I couldn't be kind and compassionate; I think I was just afraid to show it, afraid that others would perceive my kindness as weakness, a problem many men seem to have.

But after I received that devastating prognosis from my doctor that fateful day, I knew that I had never really been in a fight before. It took a few days for the news to sink in, for me to share it with my family and to learn more about this debilitating neuromuscular disorder that afflicts almost half a million Americans. But the more I read about the ways MS attacked the body, the madder I got. Suddenly, all those other things that used to set me off didn't seem like a big deal. When you're in a life-or-death grudge match with one of the orneriest opponents on the planet, you don't sweat the small stuff.

After my diagnosis, I also discovered that my most powerful weapon was not my mule-stubborn willpower, my optimistic resilience, or even my sense of humor. No, my primary line of defense was my faith in God. Suddenly, those things I'd learned in church or occasionally read or heard about in the Bible seemed to matter a whole lot more. If my life was at stake, as well as my quality of life, then I wanted to go straight to the top.

While I didn't understand why I had MS—and still don't—I couldn't believe that it was God's fault. No, I believed—and still do—that he loves me, sustains me, and strengthens me. I've been forced to trust him, and grow closer to him, in ways I never would've experienced if I didn't have MS. As strange as it sounds, I've learned to count so many blessings that have come from this unexpected physical, emotional, and mental battle. Sure, it's hard to get up every morning and grit my teeth while administering my shot of Copaxone, but it's what I have to do to stay in the fight.

I haven't fought so hard against this disease so I can live in the spotlight and make more money and win more music awards. If those things happen, great. But the reason I'm so determined to win my battle against this disorder is so I can do everything I'm called to do—especially being a good dad to my children, a loving husband to my wife, Jessie, and an honest man who treats everyone he meets the way he wants to be treated.

In other words, I like to think that I know what's worth fighting for. Those little things that used to light my short-fused temper and set me off? Well, most of them don't even cause me to think twice. I don't need to get even with someone who tries to run me off the road. I don't get upset about rude service or bad attitudes from people I encounter. I don't worry about keeping up with my peers or winning more awards or having more number one hits than anyone else. I just worry about being the best version of me that I can be. I fight to stay focused on what God calls me to do and not what will necessarily make the most money or accelerate my career.

I'm convinced that sometimes we have to drive the money changers out of our own temples and chase the temptations to sell out away from our hearts. Jesus knew what he was fighting for, and he didn't think twice about making that whip and running those merchants out of his Father's house. He demonstrated that it's more than okay to get mad and take action. We just need to be careful where we aim.

Worth Fighting For

The Bible tells us, "'In your anger do not sin': Do not let the sun go down while you are still angry, and do not give the devil a foothold" (Ephesians 4:26–27). Clearly, Jesus illustrates this balance between expressing anger and yet also not sinning. It's so tempting to stop thinking when we get

#140   03-30-2015 4:07PM
Item(s) checked out to p15092598.

TITLE: Jesus was a country boy : life le
BARCODE: 39075043665477
DUE DATE: 04-20-15

ABC Library www.abclibrary.org
Please return or renew on time 768-5170

angry and just react. It's so easy to retaliate or plan revenge on someone who's wronged us.

But harboring grudges and creating feuds is not God's way and not the kind of fighting we see Jesus engaging in. No, his message is all about forgiveness and letting go of what others have done to us. Fighting based on revenge is never going to be a fair fight. We will always lose when we're trying to get back at someone else. From Jesus's example, we see that a fair fight upholds the truth. It takes action when needed to preserve what's sacred. And it says what needs saying, no matter how hard it may be for others to hear.

The year I was diagnosed with MS, I experienced two more severe attacks and had days when I wondered if I could even get out of bed. I had moments when I found angry tears stinging my face and felt tempted to throw a pity party and give up. But there's something in me that refused to give up. After more tests and a change of doctors, I found a specialist who treated me with a new medicine designed to arrest the development of multiple sclerosis. That was almost fifteen years ago.

And in case you didn't know, I'm not in a wheelchair. I've been blessed with remarkably good health under the circumstances and have fought hard to eat well, exercise regularly, and get the rest I need. But I haven't slowed down too much. I still tour regularly, and last year I played more than a hundred shows. Most days when I'm not on the road, I'm at my farm, planting trees, plowing fields, building fences, and playing in the creek with my kids.

I've taken my fight against MS public, not only in sharing my story with my fans, but in raising awareness of this disorder to a new level. In 2003, I established Band Against MS, a nonprofit organization committed to providing education information for those living with MS and funding research toward a cure. One of the greatest achievements of my life has nothing to do with music. My efforts toward creating a world free of MS resulted in my being named Ambassador of the Year by the National Multiple Sclerosis Society in 2006, an honor they have awarded only four times in the organization's sixty-year history.

I tell you this not to brag or boast, but only to let you know that my fight goes on. The battle that began that afternoon on the basketball court when my body revealed the assault of MS is one that I continue to fight every day. But MS has not defined my life, any more than the money changers defined the temple or the Pharisees defined Jesus's ministry.

Our fights don't define us; what we're fighting for defines us.

CHAPTER THREE

Deep Roots—He Never Forgot Where He Came from . . . or Where He Was Going

Never made a ton of money

Just enough to get us by

But the things that make me rich

Is this woman and these kids of mine

You know you run into me everywhere

You need a hand, I'm gonna be right there

I'm your Average Joe

—FROM "AVERAGE JOE"

Recently my band and I were traveling on my tour bus, heading from Nashville to perform at a concert up in Pennsylvania. Usually, I don't mind traveling by bus, except for having to be away from my family—and if I'm going to be on the road for a while, I bring them with me. But most of the time, my driver pulls up in front of my house a couple hours after supper, I get on board in my sweats or pajamas, and shoot the breeze with my band guys for a while before we get in our bunks and get some sleep. When we wake up the next morning, we'll stop for coffee and a little breakfast, and the next thing you know we're there.

But on this recent road trip, it seemed as if it was taking us longer than usual to get there. I'd rested pretty well, the motion of the bus rolling up the interstate rocking me to sleep. Morning came and we hadn't stopped yet, and we still had a few more hours to go. I asked one of the guys to check the GPS to see if he could find a Starbucks coming up. Sure enough, an address for one popped up on the screen about three exits away.

We took the exit listed but didn't see a Starbucks—or really much of anything—in any direction. The all-knowing GPS told us that our beloved coffee source was about another four miles off the exit. Now I don't know if you've ever driven a forty-eight-foot motor coach, but they're not exactly the most nimble of vehicles to maneuver. But I was jonesing for my latte really bad by this point and told our driver to go for it.

Four miles down the road, still no Starbucks. We'd passed a couple of gas stations, a handful of fast-food places, and a vacant strip mall. We double-checked the address on the GPS and began checking the street address numbers along the road. When we pulled up in front of the number that was supposed to be our destination, we found a vacant warehouse. If anything, we were even farther away from Starbucks than when we started! Moral of this little wild caffeine chase? Even when you think you know where you're going, you may not know where you're going!

Lost and Found

I eventually got my latte that day, and I laugh about it now (and make sure we call ahead before stopping at anyplace located through the GPS!), but it reminds me of how easy it is to get lost. I have a pretty good sense of direction, and like most men, I don't like to stop to ask anyone for directions. Especially since I'm fortunate enough to have an electronic gadget that looks as if it belongs on a military base charting my every move on a gridded map. But as my little Starbucks detour reminded me, the wonders of almighty technology are not always as reliable as we think they are!

So often in life, we think we know where we're going, yet we end up on an unexpected detour. Sometimes we end up on the side of the road waiting for a tow truck or a mechanic to help us. Other times, we follow the directions we've received but wind up in a rural area that's nowhere close to where we want to go. Even with all our GPS systems and electronic tracking devices, we still have to pay attention to where we're going or we'll wind up someplace we don't want to be.

In the music business, it's not unusual to see talented performers lose their way and end up looking very successful while feeling very miserable. While there are many contributing factors, one that I see repeatedly is that people forget their roots. On their way up the ladder of success, they forget where they started and who they used to be. They either end up pretending to be someone they're not, or they become distracted and consumed with their success and lose sight of what's most important to them.

Like most businesses these days, in the music world you're usually only as important as your latest success. And there are always a lot of people around telling you who you should be and what you should do in order to be more successful or at least sustain the achievements you've already accomplished. Earlier in my career, I was sometimes tempted to play the personal politics of the industry and do what others told me I needed to do. If I wanted to hit the top of the charts, then my record label insisted that I do all kinds of nonpaid events sponsored by the radio stations playing my songs. If I wanted to be considered for a CMA or ACM Award, then I needed to have dinner with certain influential insiders and kiss up to them.

But those temptations faded pretty quickly. In fact, some of the best advice I ever received from country music veterans, the legendary musicians and songwriters who've earned respect along the way to their lifetime of success, was to be true to myself. So that's what I've done.

At this time in my life, I really don't know where my career is headed, but I'm not the least bit concerned about it. Maybe that's just how much my faith in God has grown over the past few years. I still work as hard as I can and do everything in my power to give 110 percent to what I love. But my life feels balanced. As much as I love music and performing, my sales numbers and awards don't define me as a man, as a husband, and as a father.

I realize it's not always easy to sit in such a sweet spot, having this kind of peace and security. It sounds deceptively simple, especially since one of the hallmarks of a true country boy is his ability to be genuine, to be real, honest, down-to-earth, grounded, and authentic. But crazy as it sounds, I've met people who worked hard to fake being genuine! In other words, they tried to come across as country but only as long as it allowed them to get what they wanted.

They were just putting on an act, and no matter what act you're putting on, if you're not living with integrity and being who you really are, then you're missing out. You're living a lie and depriving those around you from what you genuinely could give them if you weren't so busy trying to be something, or someone, else. All of us will face opportunities and temptations to be someone other than who we are. But as we see in the life of the greatest Country Boy who ever lived, when you know who you are, it's easy to know where you're going.

A Way in a Manger

In my humble opinion, one of the main reasons that Jesus's ministry was so effective stems from the fact that he remained true to his upbringing. He grew up in a working-class home and wasn't afraid to get his hands dirty. He hung out with fishermen and tax collectors, prostitutes and foreigners. He appreciated the power of a good story as well as the importance of respecting the land. From the very beginning of his life, Jesus was close to animals and loved looking up at his Father's handiwork in the stars above his head. His life wasn't about power and pretense, material possessions and fame. His path began with a way in a manger.

One of the things I love most about Christmastime is seeing a nativity scene. Whether it's large or small, homemade or store bought, crafted by an artist or made by a child out of Play-Doh, there's just something special about the image of Mary and Joseph and the Baby Jesus huddled together under the shelter of what must've been something like a run-down barn. It's ironic, even, that we often get caught up in spending a lot of money and trying to have the brightest lightest or the flashiest tree when that original Christmas scene could not have been more country.

As we've already touched on, most everything about Jesus threw people for a loop. It's almost as if God deliberately wanted to mess with everyone's expectations just to make his point very clear. Prophets and religious leaders had anticipated the birth of the Messiah for hundreds of years, and by the time Jesus was born in Bethlehem, it was natural that people were expecting it to be a really big deal. After all, this was the Son of God! Surely, he would be born into a royal palace with all the trappings, right?

Nope. As you're probably aware, instead of being born in Jerusalem or any other important Jewish city at the time, Jesus was born in a little back-road sheep town. "While they were there, the time came for the baby to be born, and she gave birth to her firstborn, a son. She wrapped him in cloths and placed him in a manger, because there was no guest room available for them" (Luke 2:6–7). This town was so small that when Caesar Augustus declared a census to be taken and everyone to return to the place of his family's origin, Joseph could not find a place to stay. There was no room at the inn and apparently not that many inns to be found. As it turns out, he may have felt fortunate even to have a corner of an old barn.

And instead of a golden, jewel-encrusted crib, Jesus was born in a dirty old manger, the one that some cows and sheep had probably eaten from only a couple of hours earlier. There was no royal fanfare or public announcement; instead, there was the sound of animals and angels appearing to some nearby shepherds. When three kings from the East did come looking for this newborn king, they had to follow a star, not a palace road map.

In fact, the reigning monarch, King Herod, was so worried and threatened by the rumors he'd heard about a new king being born that he ordered all baby boys to be killed. The three wise men were able to warn Joseph, who then took his little family down into Egypt until Herod died and the coast was clear. Not only was Jesus not born into a rich, royal situation, but he had to leave the country for his own safety. Curiously enough, it's the people in power who were usually threatened by Jesus, the religious leaders like the

Pharisees, or insecure leaders like Herod. It's the shepherds and fishermen who end up being drawn to Jesus for his genuine sense of authority, compassion, and wisdom.

Down by the River

We don't know a lot about what it was like for Jesus growing up. We know that he visited the temple when he was around twelve years old and ended up teaching the teachers there a few things. We know that after his parents returned with him from Egypt they lived in Nazareth, where his father was a carpenter. It seems likely that Jesus helped out in his father's woodshop, handing him tools, holding planks of olive wood while Joseph sawed them.

Before he finally began his public ministry, Jesus went through a personal initiation and time of preparation. He went to his cousin, John the Baptist, and asked to be baptized, despite John's protests that he wasn't worthy to baptize the Son of God. So they head off to the Jordan River, where something incredibly noteworthy takes place. "As soon as Jesus was baptized, he went up out of the water. At that moment heaven was opened, and he saw the Spirit of God descending like a dove and alighting on him. And a voice from heaven said, 'This is my Son, whom I love; with him I am well pleased'" (Matthew 3:16–17).

It was almost like a commencement, the ceremony we have to celebrate when someone graduates from high school or college. We celebrate the accomplishment and launch him into the next season of his life. Here we see God looking down and saying, "Son, I'm proud of you! I'm so glad you're my boy! I love you, son." Whether he admits it or not, every country boy wants his daddy's blessing, wants to be recognized and respected as a full-grown man and no longer a little kid. It's not that Jesus didn't know who he was or that his Father loved him before this event, but it sure didn't hurt to experience that gift.

Interestingly enough, right after he was given a nice "attaboy!," Jesus found his identity attacked. After being baptized in the Jordan by John the Baptist, Jesus went off to the desert to be alone with his Father. He fasted forty days there and then returned to begin his public ministry. Obviously, this time was a crucial juncture in his life and a pivotal point in his fulfilling his divine mission.

So it should be no surprise then that he was about to experience an intense encounter with temptation. Who should be waiting to tempt him as he returns from the desert? The enemy, of course, talking smoother than a lawyer selling silk! (check out Matthew 4:1–11). I've found that we often face the most grueling temptations when we are coming off a time of feeling close to God. It may be after an event or retreat or it may simply be a time when you're exhausted from gladly serving others in some way. This seems to be a prime time for us to be tempted to forget who we are.

Hunger Games

Jesus faced three separate temptations when he faced the devil in the desert. First, the enemy took advantage of Christ's physical hunger—after all, he'd been fasting for forty days—and tempted him to turn stones into bread. This strategy seems to be one our enemy uses frequently— exploiting our physical appetites. With Adam and Eve in the Garden of Eden, it was an apple. When Jacob tricked his brother out of his birthright, he used a bowl of stew as bait. Now with Jesus, it was fresh bread.

When we're feeling hungry, tired, depressed, lonely, or aroused, it's not easy to remember who we are and what we're about. If we're so consumed by hunger or thirst— either literally or just for some goal of ours, by greed or lust to attain something or someone, then we can lose sight of the commitments we've made and the responsibilities we have. When our appetites get the best of us, we often forget where we came from and where we're going. It's a lot easier to focus on the immediate gratification that comes from getting what will taste good or feel good right away—even if ultimately it's not good for us.

When I'm on tour or performing on the road, it sometimes feels like I'm in another world. Everything revolves around me and what I want and how I want it. At the same time, it's not about me as a person so much as it's about me as a commodity, a business generator, a performer. Routines get out of whack, and it's all a little disorienting and eventually very draining.

Fortunately, I learned my limits pretty quickly, especially after my battle with MS began. But it's not just my health I'm concerned about that keeps me coming home. Nothing grounds me like my wife and kids. Recently, I flew home after being in Phoenix for a few days. It was raining pretty hard when we landed, a nice summer shower. When I pulled into our driveway, I couldn't believe what I saw! Jessie and our kids were decked out in rain jackets, dancing, splashing, and eagerly waiting to welcome me home! I couldn't wait to join them, and pretty soon we were all soaked but happier than you can imagine. This is what keeps me grounded.

Nowadays, I stop and think long and hard before I accept

a show or agree to an event or anything that will pull me away from home. My grounding comes not only from my being with my family but also from my being engaged with them—playing with the kids, reading them bedtime stories, cooking dinner with Jess, curling up for a good movie after putting the kids to bed. There's nothing in the world that I enjoy more than these moments. And remembering how blessed I am to have so many wonderful people in my life keeps me focused on what matters most.

I'm convinced that too often people give in to temptation because they lose sight of the big picture for their lives. They feel so overwhelmed by immediate pain or disappointment that they compromise and take a shortcut for a few minutes of comfort or relief. But God wants more for us than what we often settle for in the heat of the moment.

He wants our commitment and dedication to him to be stronger than the physical sensations of our own bodies. He wants us to have a larger perspective in order to meet our soul's deeper hunger. Just as Jesus gave Living Water to quench the thirst of the Samaritan woman at the well, God wants to nourish more than just our bodies. He wants us to remember who we are and not be distracted by the shiny objects we encounter along our path.

Or think about it this way. You remember what it feels like when you're infatuated with someone? You're just falling in love, and you seem to lose touch with everything unrelated to the object of your affection. You're not hungry, and you can't sleep. You're so in love that you feel good only when you're with your beloved. This is the kind of passion God wants from us.

And this is the message that Jesus uses to rebuke Satan and turn down his offer: the Word of God provides much more nourishment for us than bread ever can. We are not merely animals reduced to our appetites. We are created in the image of God and have eternal souls. Our ultimate need for a changed life, for renewal and redemption, trumps our temporary hunger for a biscuit or piece of corn bread!

Power Play

Next the devil goes for a direct assault on Jesus's identity: "Well, since you're the Son of God, then prove it and jump!" He baits the Savior by taunting him with showing off. "If you're really who you say you are, then show me!" Talk about trying to pick a fight—I don't think the Hatfields and the McCoys were that direct!

Have you ever had someone challenge your identity or question the person you know yourself to be?

My experiences in the super-competitive music industry taught me very quickly that there were plenty of people who wanted to kick me down a few levels and keep me in what they saw as my place.

When things don't go your way, when you have someone in your face, saying, "Who do you think you are? What makes you so special?," it can be hard to remain confident. It's always easier to conform to others' expectations and demands. But conforming at the cost of being who you really are will only make you miserable, no matter how much money you have in the bank or the number of awards you have on the shelf.

Similarly, our identities are often attacked, and we're challenged to question who we are as God's children. The devil likes to get in our heads and play on our insecurities and weaknesses. "You're not God's child—if you were, then you wouldn't steal money from your clients." "You're nothing like Christ—if you were a real believer, then you wouldn't gossip about your coworkers at the office." We can fill in the blank with whatever chronic struggles we may often face. The devil wants to use those against us even though God has said that in Christ we are new creatures, forgiven and redeemed. Because of the cross, he no longer sees our sin but only the image of his perfect Son who died in our place.

Once again, Jesus let the devil have it by responding with

the truth of God's Word, which says that we're not to test God. In other words, Jesus chose to believe what his Father said was true about himself rather than what this smooth-talking bully was trying to sell. When our thoughts are anchored in the Bible, we won't lose sight of our true identities when the devil—or anybody else—tries to plant doubt or accusations in our mind.

You Can Have It All

Finally, the third temptation that the devil uses to try to sideline Jesus involves the world on a platter. He took Christ to a mountaintop and showed him all the kingdoms of the world and everything they offered—power, wealth, fame, authority, sex, dominion over everything and everyone. Basically, Jesus could have anything in this world that his heart desired. The only condition was to bow down and worship the enemy, the ultimate idol, the prince of lies.

Jesus didn't buy the devil's offer and neither should we. Christ replied that it's God and God alone whom we should worship and serve. We must remember that we belong to God and that nothing else we encounter in this world will ever satisfy us. This truth should be a cornerstone in the foundation of our hearts. If we can remember who we really are as God's children, as followers of Jesus, and if we can remember that we are more than just our appetites, then we will not give in to any temptations that come our way.

After winning this smackdown with Satan in the desert, Jesus must have felt more confident than ever before in who he was and where he was going. He embraced and exercised the power and authority that came from being the Son of God, but he never became boastful, proud, or arrogant. He surprised people with his kindness and gentleness. And he also wasn't afraid to tick people off, as we saw in the last chapter.

Reap What You Sow

Now I need to give a disclaimer here, one that I hope was clear in my introduction. I'm not worthy to write a book about God. I'm not a pastor, scholar, theology professor, or Bible expert. I'm just a good old country boy who tries to stay focused on the only perfect person who ever walked this earth: Jesus. I'm just as fallible as the next person out there, but I do realize that God loves us even more than we love the children in our lives. Whether it's our own kids, our nieces and nephews, or just children for whom we're baby-sitting, we want to help them, correct them, and keep them focused on the very best things for their lives.

In the same way, God wants to instruct us as his children and guide our lives with his wisdom. Jesus used his encounters with people as teaching moments, opportunities to surprise them with God's truth. While his message may have surprised his listeners at times, he always drew on situations that were familiar and accessible to his audience. In fact, many of Jesus's most effective teaching moments came out of the stories he would tell, parables, that drew on his knowledge—and his audience's familiarity—with farming and an agrarian lifestyle. One of my favorites takes place immediately after Jesus has just delivered the Sermon on the Mount:

Again Jesus began to teach by the lake. The crowd that gathered around him was so large that he got into a boat and sat in it out on the lake, while all the people were along the shore at the water's edge. He taught them many things by parables, and in his teaching said: "Listen! A farmer went out to sow his seed. As he was scattering the seed, some fell along the path, and the birds came and ate it up. Some fell on rocky places, where it did not have much soil. It sprang up quickly, because the soil was shallow. But when the sun came up, the plants were scorched, and they withered because they had no root. Other seed fell among thorns, which grew up and choked the plants, so that they did not bear grain. Still other seed fell on good soil. It came up, grew and produced a crop, some multiplying thirty, some sixty, some a hundred times."

Then Jesus said, "Whoever has ears to hear, let them hear." (Mark 4:1–9)

Instead of telling his listeners that they must allow God's love to grow in their lives, he gave them a much more concrete and vivid picture. Something they could relate to instantly and had probably seen before: a farmer sowing his seeds at planting time. This illustration is something most country boys and girls can still relate to, even if they're using a John Deere or International Harvester instead of a seed bag and hand plow.

How Does Your Garden Grow

I know I sure can. Growing up in the country, my family lived off the land and relied on having a vegetable garden most years when I was growing up. My daddy had an old rototiller that he'd used to plow up the big rectangle we'd designated as "the garden patch." It was always amazing to watch the earth turn into neat rows of brown furrows. Then we'd plant the seeds that we'd saved, had been given by neighbors, or had bought in town at the co-op feed store. We had rows of squash, cucumbers, red potatoes, onions, pole beans, pumpkins, some tomato plants, and a few rows of corn on the far side.

I learned quickly and at a young age how much work it takes to maintain a healthy garden. Sometimes there was no rain for weeks, so I would have to haul three connecting hoses from the outdoor faucet on the side of the house to make sure everything got enough water. A few times, de-spite our best efforts, we still had the corn get burned up. In-stead of tall green stalks with nice fat ears of corn, we ended up with brown, withered sticks that looked like overgrown weeds. One year, I didn't plant the seeds deep enough, and crows and chickens ate up most of the seed. And if we didn't hoe and weed the garden almost every day, then we knew that we'd end up with plenty of kudzu and mustard grass but no vegetables.

In telling his parable, Jesus drew on all these scenarios to convey the various possibilities we experience when we encounter God in our lives. Some people ignore him and their faith evaporates as they get distracted and consumed by other goals. Other people find their faith withered by the heat of life's trials and circumstances. Still others find their hearts choked by the mistakes and selfish decisions they've made. In each instance, God's love has no room to grow.

However, sometimes the seed takes root and produces a bountiful harvest—Jesus says up to a hundred times that one original seed. I can remember a few summers having squash running out our ears, and our neighbors would often bring us cucumbers or tomatoes because their garden had produced more than they could use. When we allow God to work in our lives, we enjoy a harvest that's more bountiful than anything we could accomplish on our own.

True Blue

By choosing examples that his listeners would find familiar, Jesus stayed true to his country boy roots. Sure, he could have chosen examples from history or literature, from classical poetry or great Jewish leaders. But he wasn't trying to impress people with his knowledge or dazzle them with his command of factual data. He simply wanted to get his point across in a way that was memorable, accessible, and clear. So he chose something both he and his audience knew well—planting seeds.

When I'm writing a song, I try to follow the same strategy. It can be tempting to create a flowery melody or a catchy refrain, but if the song doesn't say something, if it doesn't share a story or convey genuine emotion or insight into living, then it's not going to last. I wouldn't be true to myself and the fans of the kind of music I make if I wrote classical music with lyrics in Italian. That's called opera, I believe, and while I appreciate it and find it beautiful, ultimately, it's not who I am or what I'm about as a songwriter.

I'm proud of my many accomplishments and grateful that I get to make a successful living doing what I love. But I'm also thankful for the lessons I learned growing up and struggling. I'm not ashamed of where I started and know that it will all influence who I am and the choices I make. No matter where I live, how much money I make, or the number of chart-topping songs I have, I'm still Clay Walker from Beaumont, Texas.

Country boys and country gals never lose sight of their roots, even if they grew up hard and experienced some painful struggles. They're never ashamed of their origins, whether they're from a small town or the inner city. They learned that being true to themselves means remaining humble, resourceful, and resilient.

No matter how successful they become, they never lose sight of the lessons learned when growing up. The importance of family. The importance of keeping their word. Of looking someone in the eye and offering their hand. Staying true to his small-town roots, Jesus never wavered from his purpose of pointing people back to his Father's love. He reminds us to remain grounded even as we shoot for the stars, to remember where we came from while chasing our dreams.

Jesus Knew How to LAUGH

★

CHAPTER FOUR

Happy Hours—He Knew How to Have a Good Time

I don't wanna think about tomorrow
I don't need anything money can buy
I don't have to beg, steal, or borrow
I just wanna live until I die
—FROM "LIVE UNTIL I DIE"

Recently, I attended a party to celebrate a big country music awards event. It was a black-tie gala held in a spacious facility that had been decorated to look as if we were outside under the stars. Ladies wore fancy designer gowns, and the guys wore boots with their tuxes. My wife had never looked more beautiful, and we were both amazed to see a number of music superstars with names you'd recognize.

As we mingled and greeted other people there, caterers served gourmet appetizers and drinks. Later, a delicious meal was served, prepared by a team of executive chefs. A five-piece band played softly from the back of the room, the place settings at our table were bejeweled to look like stars in the night sky, and fresh flowers bloomed from enormous vases. Luxury gift bags had been prepared with all kinds of goodies to take home.

While I loved seeing friends and fellow country music lovers there, as far as parties go . . . well, I was bored. Everyone seemed polite and reserved, talking softly, saying the right things to their companion of the moment before moving on to someone else to repeat the process. People seemed very self-conscious and afraid to do anything that might attract attention. There was a little dance floor set up over by the band, but nobody danced. The food was pretty and tasted good, but I had no idea who had prepared it.

Anyone looking in would have probably been envious and thought that this was the party to end all parties. And yet I was eager to get it over with and go home. Many of the ingredients were there, but something vital was still missing.

As I thought about it, I realized that these formal events are rarely a true down-home-party kind of celebration. Because when I think of really enjoying myself with friends and family, it's usually a lot looser. We love to have people come out to our farm and have a great meal and just enjoy themselves. I like to barbecue and grill and just relax and have a great time. We usually invite our friends and their families and always welcome whomever they want to bring as well. The more the merrier, we always say!

It's totally informal, sometimes spontaneous, and always memorable. It's the times when you're having a cold beer and talking with buddies about fishing and where you'll take the kids this summer. It's the get-togethers where you end up telling funny stories about your childhood and where you're from. Everyone's joking and just kicking back, catching up, going back for more baked beans, grabbing some chips, and pouring another cold drink. Kids are usually running around, chasing one another, spilling lemonade, and feeding potato salad to the dogs in the yard. These kinds of get-togethers feel spontaneous, unplanned, alive, and awake. People don't feel pressured to do anything other than relax and have another piece of pie. These are the kind of cookouts we like to have out at our farm whenever we get the chance.

What makes the difference between these two kinds of gatherings? How can an event with lavish food and a beautiful setting end up being such a dud? And how can a thrown-together backyard gathering with hot dogs and stale chips be so much fun? Well, it can only be the people in attendance and their ability to celebrate.

Here Comes the Bride

One of the events where you can really tell if people know how to celebrate is, of course, a wedding. Like many performers, I played a lot of different gigs while my career was getting off the ground. Weddings were always my favorite, maybe because I'm such a sentimental kind of guy, or maybe because it's always a great place to sing love songs.

And each wedding is incredibly different. I've sung at friends' weddings with only a few dozen family and friends gathered in someone's backyard. And I've performed in massive reception halls with a full band and hundreds of people in attendance.

I've seen beautiful women walk down the aisle in dresses that cost more than my first new pickup truck. And I've seen simple ceremonies with couples holding wildflowers on a hillside. One wedding I attended was particularly memorable. It was held outdoors at a beautiful ranch, and the bride and groom rode in on horseback. The weather was perfect, and everything was going smoothly until the groom's stallion was hit by a call of nature. Nothing like the smell of manure right in the middle of your wedding vows to seal the deal! Only in Texas, right?

In almost every wedding I've attended, though, it seems like someone there is worried about all the details.

It may be the bride, or her mother, or the wedding planner, or Aunt Thelma, but someone there is stressed out about whether the little boy who's ring bearer will trip and lose the ring. Or whether the flowers will start to wilt. Or whether the band will show up for the reception. Or whether the wedding cake will taste good. Or how they're going to pay for it all!

To our knowledge, Jesus never officiated at anyone's wedding, but he sure did make a splash at one. After he had been baptized and called his disciples, but before he'd started his public ministry, Jesus found himself at a wedding in the town of Cana. Some scholars think that he may even have been distantly related to the bride or groom since his mother, Mary, attended as well. In any case, he ended up performing his first public miracle and making the reception a country-boy kind of celebration.

Wedding Crashers

Now even in Jesus's time, weddings relied on all the details coming together. And they did it not just for one day, but for an entire week! Couples then didn't go on a Caribbean cruise for their honeymoon or register their china pattern at a department store, but they definitely had a heap of expectations on them.

For a Jewish wedding in Jesus's day, the couple would've been treated like royalty for seven days. The wedding ceremony itself took place on the third day of this special week, but afterward the couple did not leave to go on their honeymoon. Instead, they and their families would host a lavish celebration with as many family, friends, acquaintances, and local religious leaders as possible.

In fact, it was considered rude to turn away anyone who wanted to attend. There was no such thing as wedding crashers! People didn't even have to know the bride and groom to be invited. Celebrating the new union properly was simply an expected, cultural obligation. It was a matter of family honor and public reputation.

With both the bride's and groom's respective families involved, they shared the responsibility to provide the food and wine over this extended period and to make sure that all the attendees had everything they wanted to eat and drink. The worst thing that could happen would be to run out of food or to drain the last wine jug while guests were still around. Just think about having to cook, serve, and clean for hundreds of guests for over four days!

With this kind of situation in mind, let's see how Jesus

found himself transforming something ordinary into something no one would ever forget.

On the third day a wedding took place at Cana in Galilee. Jesus' mother was there, and Jesus and his disciples had also been invited to the wedding. When the wine was gone, Jesus' mother said to him, "They have no more wine."

"Woman, why do you involve me?" Jesus replied. "My hour has not yet come."

His mother said to the servants, "Do whatever he tells you."

Nearby stood six stone water jars, the kind used by the Jews for ceremonial washing, each holding from twenty to thirty gallons.

Jesus said to the servants, "Fill the jars with water"; so they filled them to the brim.

Then he told them, "Now draw some out and take it to the master of the banquet."

They did so, and the master of the banquet tasted the water that had been turned into wine. He did not realize where it had come from, though the servants who had drawn the water knew. Then he called the bridegroom aside and said, "Everyone brings out the choice wine first and then the cheaper wine after the guests have had too much to drink; but you have saved the best till now." (John 2:1–10)

Okay, so Jesus and his disciples are attending this shindig, and since Mary, his mom, was also there, it seems logical (and supported by historians, as I mentioned) that they were related to either the bride's family or the groom's. Maybe it was one of those situations we've all been in before, something like: "Come on, now—it's your cousin Cheryl's wedding. Yes, you do have to go! And you're going to have a good time!"

Family events mattered then just as they matter now, and a wedding is definitely one to celebrate. There are certain family obligations that transcend heaven and earth. My wife's cousin recently got married, and even with traveling with the kids, changing everyone's routines, and rescheduling some of my concerts, we wouldn't have missed it for the world. As challenging as it was to make the time to get there, it was the highlight of our summer. We loved connecting with family members we hadn't seen in a long time and just enjoying the opportunity to celebrate together.

Wine List

So whether Jesus wanted to be there or found he was obligated to attend, he was there. And this Jewish wedding celebration was going full throttle and the village of Cana was rocking. We're told it's the third day, which means it was the third day after the wedding ceremony, so the wonderful wedding week was coming to an end. At long last, the bride and groom were hitched, everyone who's anyone was there, and the party was about to wind up. And then, apparently, Mary found out, probably discreetly from one of the other ladies there, that they'd just run out of wine. So like any good mother, what does she do? She went to get her boy, who just happened to be the Son of God, to take care of it!

Now what I love about this story is the interaction between mother and son here. Notice that Mary doesn't *ask* Jesus to do something about the problem. Nor does she tell him he has to do something. She just passes along an important piece of info: "They're out of wine."

And how does her son respond? "So? What do you want me to do? It's not like it's time to let everyone know about . . . well, you know." Even though he's probably around thirty years old, Jesus's response makes me smile as I remember being a teenager and rolling my eyes at some of the things my parents forced me to do. In fact, forgive me for taking liberties with the translation here, but I think Jesus was really asking, "Mom, do you really want to risk blowing my cover and God's sense of timing by having me come up with some wine here at the end of this little country wedding?"

So what happened? Now, this is where you just have to love the situation. Maybe this incident is in the Bible just to remind sons always to do what their mamas tell them! Scripture doesn't give us a recorded response from Mary following her son's reply, and I'm convinced it's because she didn't say a word. She didn't have to!

If you're a parent, then you get this immediately—sometimes you just don't have the energy to argue with your son or daughter over what they need to do. And as the sons and daughters of dear mothers ourselves, then we've probably been on the receiving end of at least one of these silent conversations. You know, the kind where even though no words are uttered, a whole lot of communication takes place!

I suspect Mary gave Jesus "the look": the one every mother naturally knows how to employ to get her child to do something he may not want to do. Whether you've given one or received one, or both, you know the look I'm talking about. I can remember being a teenager and my mom telling me that an elderly lady at church, Mrs. Wilson, didn't have anyone to mow her yard for her.

"That's too bad," I said, trying my best to sound sincere. Mom didn't say a word but just tilted her head down a little and looked at me. Her eyes seemed to be saying, *Really? Do you really want to make this harder than it has to be for both of us? Now go over there and get that yard cut!* I maintained eye contact for a couple moments and then agreed to get the job done.

All Mary had to do was give Jesus "the look" to silently communicate that he'd better get busy and "just do it!" She looked at him, he got it, and then Mary turned to the servants and said, "Whatever he says to do, you do it." Once again, just do it (maybe the Nike guys were inspired by this story). And so they did.

Trust and Obey

Notice that the servants obeyed both Mary's command ("Do whatever he says to do!") as well as the very specific instructions that Jesus then gave them. He said to fill the water jugs to the brim with water. So they took six of these huge, ceremonial containers, each about twenty-five gallons, and filled them up with water. They did what he asked them to do, exactly as he requested. They didn't pour olive oil into one and goat's milk into another. They didn't fill them half full. Jesus said to the brim, so that's exactly what they did.

Sometimes I wonder if we take only the parts of God's instruction that're convenient or make sense or seem logical to obey and throw out the rest. And I'm not saying that we should try to handle snakes or take dangerous risks; I'm just thinking that a lot of what doesn't seem clear to us is crystal from God's point of view. I suspect there are many times when he wants to bless us, but we get in the way of receiving his gifts because we're not willing to be obedient in the small things.

Many times we know what needs to be done but don't do it. Worried about money? Then make sure you give it away. Afraid of never finding, or of losing, a spouse? Then love God first. Concerned about staying healthy? Then dedicate your body as the temple of God's Spirit in you. When the focus shifts from worry to obedience, the things that cause us to worry in the first place often go away.

Because when we're obedient, we discover that our actions have been transformed by God's power into something bigger, better, richer, more dynamic than we could've imagined. Obedience transforms our beliefs into life-giving faith, just like Jesus transforms water into wine. Water is essential for us to live; our bodies are made mostly of water.

Similarly, all of us believe something; it's impossible to go through life without beliefs—even if our belief is in nothing! When our faith is put into action, then it becomes dynamic and life-giving, full of flavor and power. Every drop of water placed in those huge jugs was transformed into a drop of the most delicious wine.

Many times we know what needs to be done in those areas of worry and yet we don't do them. If we're worried about money, then we need to think about being a steward of God's resources and not making money an idol. Sometimes we make idols out of something we don't have just as much as something we have too much of.

Afraid of being alone or lonely? Afraid of never finding, or of losing, a spouse? Then love God first and treat the people around you with respect and kindness. Worried about being healthy and getting and staying in shape? Then make your habits work for you—what you eat, how you exercise, and how much rest you get.

So many of the little concerns and the big worries disappear when we obey God and trust him to handle the outcomes of these areas of our life. When the focus shifts from worry to obedience, the things that caused us to worry in the first place often go away. Because when we're obedi-ent, we discover that our actions have been transformed by God's power into something bigger, better, more powerful, more purposeful than we could've imagined.

The Best for Last

Certainly the families of the bride and groom that day in Cana discovered that they could let their worries go because God was present and in charge. I love the end of this story, as the wine that Jesus has just created is taken to the master of the banquet to sample. This guy was probably some local religious leader they were obligated to invite who got to oversee the party and sample everything first. He was being honored even as his presence honored the happy couple.

Just as a waiter in a nice restaurant will pour a little wine in your glass for you to smell and taste before he serves ev-eryone, this dignitary at Cana got to sample the wedding wine. Can't you just imagine this scene? He gets the first glass of this very unique vintage and can't believe how good it tastes! Little did he know that it was only five minutes old, not five years!

Since he obviously didn't know where the wine came

from, he found the bridegroom and paid the ultimate compliment. "What an amazing host! Thank you for saving your best wine to serve last! Most people use the good wine first, and then after everyone's had a few glasses, they bring out the cheap stuff. Not you—you're a class act! You're just now serving the most delicious wine I've ever tasted." Not only had Jesus (or perhaps I should say Mary, since she's the one who got the ball rolling) prevented the wedding party from being embarrassed, but he had brought them great honor and prestige in the eyes of their guests.

I love the fact that Jesus's first public miracle was not raising someone from the dead, healing someone's illness, or casting demons out of them. It was simply blessing a family and celebrating with them. It was saving them embarrassment on a day when they were celebrating a new covenant between their two families. It was removing worry and replacing it with joy. It was making a wedding a party they would remember for a long time.

Time Out

Country folks know what it means to slow down and take life as it comes. They know how to be spontaneous and enjoy life in the present moment. They understand how to put life's worries aside and appreciate all the blessings God has given them.

One of my favorite episodes of the old Andy Griffith show revolves around a busy city businessman who has car trouble while passing through Mayberry. Because it's a Sunday, Wally's filling station is closed, and Goober can't repair his car until the next day. Andy brings the man back home for Sunday dinner, of course, where Aunt Bea cooks up a feast. After the delicious, home-cooked meal, they sit on the porch and talk for a spell before Andy pulls out his guitar and they sing a few songs.

The city slicker finds himself suddenly forced to slow down and enjoy life in a way that he no longer allows himself to do. In fact, as a favor, Goober ends up fixing the man's car that afternoon so that he can be on his way and keep his important meeting the next morning. However, the man's attitude has changed so much that he finds something else wrong with his car just so he can stay and enjoy a few more hours of hospitality.

Like so many episodes of this classic series, there's a timeless, powerful lesson beneath the jokes and southern drawls. Now more than ever, we are bombarded with thousands of choices every day. From where we get our news to which of the hundreds of products advertised before our eyes we should purchase to how we'll spend our time doing what we "must" do, most of us experience life in a blurred pace of constant motion. We forget to take time out to enjoy what we have. We lose sight of slowing down, resting, relaxing, and celebrating with the people we love.

The more our busy lives get hijacked by technology, other people's expectations, and all the demands on our time, the more we need time by ourselves. There're usually so many distractions and diversions, entertainments and information bombarding us that we forget how good it can feel to be alone with ourselves and God. I think we need to know how to celebrate our own time alone with God before we can know how to extend it to a party with other people.

One of the ways I love to experience this kind of solitude is at a little place I have down in Galveston on the beach. I grew up saltwater fishing and have so many wonderful memories of days when I would just be on the water, watching the current, feeling the sun warm my skin, hearing the waves splash hypnotically. I like to take my old fishing boat out in the Gulf and just find a spot that's nothing but blue.

About forty, fifty, sixty miles offshore, I'll stop the boat and just cast out into the cobalt water. The wind calms down, and the water gets so still and peaceful. Sometimes

I'll be on the water at sunrise and watch the first pink kiss of the sun along the cheek of the horizon. I can describe it, but I can't explain it. Cell phones don't work. No Internet. Just tranquillity. Beauty. God's presence.

Jesus knew what this kind of personal celebration, this kind of worship, was all about. He, too, loved the water and enjoyed fishing. He knew he needed time away with his Father if he was to continue his ministry and be a fisher of men. He knew what it meant to let go of his worries.

Thou Shalt Not Worry

Without a doubt, Jesus made it very clear that we're wasting precious moments when we worry. And greater still, we're unnecessarily undermining our faith in the Father who loves us so much that he's going to take care of everything we need. Let's look at how he responded to the worriers of his day.

Then Jesus said to his disciples: "Therefore I tell you, do not worry about your life, what you will eat; or about your body, what you will wear. For life is more than food, and the body more than clothes. Consider the ravens: They do not sow or reap, they have no storeroom or barn; yet God feeds them. And how much more valuable you are than birds! Who of you by worrying can add a single hour to your life? Since you cannot do this very little thing, why do you worry about the rest?

"Consider how the wild flowers grow. They do not labor or spin. Yet I tell you, not even Solomon in all his splendor was dressed like one of these. If that is how God clothes the grass of the field, which is here today, and tomorrow is thrown into the fire, how much more will he clothe you—you of little faith! And do not set your heart on what you will eat or drink; do not worry about it. For the pagan world runs after all such things, and your Father knows that you need them. But seek his kingdom, and these things will be given to you as well."
(Luke 12:22–31)

Now, right off the bat, it's important that we realize here that Jesus is not just giving us some friendly advice or a helpful hint—it's a command. This isn't a nice little slogan ("Don't worry—be happy!") that we can put on a bumper sticker or a coffee mug. As surprising as it might sound, this is clearly an order. He doesn't begin by saying, "Maybe you should think about . . ." or "It might help you if . . ." No, he says, plain as day: "Do not worry." Which implies that we have a choice about whether to worry or not. So many people seem to assume that worrying is just part of their nature, an aspect of their personality, just something they can't help. But Jesus makes it clear here that we're not off the hook so easily.

Not only are we not to worry but Jesus clearly commands us not to be consumed with worrying about what we're going to eat and what we're going to wear today. Isn't it good to know that even in Jesus's day, kids were probably asking their mothers, "What's for supper?" And wives were probably going into their closets and sighing, "I don't have a thing to wear."

And it's funny, but if you think about it, obeying Jesus's command not to worry about food and clothes would wipe out the majority of reality shows on TV! The Food Network wouldn't exist, and neither would shows like *What Not to Wear*, *Project Runway*, or *Say Yes to the Dress*.

Eat, Drink, and Be Merry

Joking aside, it's good to keep in mind that when people worried about what to eat in Jesus's day, they were usually worried about *if* they would eat that day. This is the nation of Israel that survived a seven-year famine by heading down to Egypt, a move that saved their lives but resulted in captivity. Then God used Moses to lead them out of slavery and into the Promised Land, providing manna along the way so they wouldn't starve in the desert. These are people who go out for the day with their families to hear Jesus deliver the Sermon on the Mount and not take any food with them, resulting in the first church picnic ever recorded—even if it was fish sandwiches for everyone.

Unless you were in the small minority of the wealthy, most people got by day to day, fortunate if they had flour to make bread and clean water to drink. They didn't go to Walmart or Kroger to stock up their fridge in case friends dropped by for a cookout. No, each day was often a struggle, a challenge to find food or to work and earn enough to buy or barter what they needed. The nearest well with fresh water—remember, Israel is an arid, desert climate—was often miles away. As we see in Jesus's encounter with the Samaritan woman at the well, drawing water was a daily chore for most households.

Certainly, hunger is still an issue for us today, as well as, in so many parts of the world, having clean water. Because our bodies need constant nourishment and hydration, Jesus knew that people would always be worrying about what to eat and drink, no matter how much food they might have. He knows it's human nature.

So knowing that the daily worry that some people have for food and water is real and urgent, Jesus was not being insensitive by telling his listeners, as well as us today, "Do not worry." It may seem counterintuitive not to worry about something as essential as nourishment for your body, but he tells us that God will take care of us. He says, "Look at the birds—those ravens over there! They're not farming and storing food, and yet they have plenty to eat. If God cares enough to provide food for them, then you know he'll do the same for you."

If you've ever seen any, then you know ravens are one ugly bird. Black and kind of creepy-looking, they're basically scavengers. So by pointing out the ravens, Jesus chose something that his audience would find familiar and not that likable. But his point was clear: if God makes sure that even the ravens are fed without their doing a single thing, then surely he'll take care of us. We are his children, created in his image. He's going to provide for us.

Jesus goes on to tell us, similarly, that we shouldn't worry about what we wear. Now, for a lot of country boys, this command is a no-brainer. They're never worrying about what to wear—they just throw on a pair of jeans, a T-shirt, boots, and a cap. But this part of the do-not-worry command is more than just a matter of vanity, although that's addressed as well.

Just as food is essential to the body, we must protect

ourselves from the elements with the clothing we wear. This is especially true in the desert, where blistering temperatures can burn uncovered skin in less than an hour, and where temperatures drop dramatically when the sun goes down. If you've ever been camping and tried to sleep in freezing weather with a sleeping bag that felt more like a fishnet, then you know how important it can be to be covered up.

But not only does God make sure we have clothes to wear, but we can know that we look just as beautiful as the lilies that grow wild in the fields. Jesus says that even Solomon, one of the richest men who ever lived, couldn't dress as splendidly as the lilies. For us, it's a good reminder that the fanciest designers can't outdo the beauty and complexity of a wildflower, something that we don't even plant. Jesus tells us that worrying about clothes—whether we have clothes and what our clothes look like—is a waste of time.

God cares about the small details of our life so we don't have to worry about them. He understands that we want to know how we'll pay for our kids' college education or how we'll afford another vehicle when our spouse goes back to work. He cares that we want the best health care for our aging parents or that we need to get our roof repaired after the storm. But worrying about these things or about anything else in our lives is not the key to living an authentic life of faith, a life of joy and peace and fulfillment.

When we obey God and put our faith in action, we trust that he will provide for us. We know that we can relax and slow down and take time to enjoy everything we have. We can appreciate the people we love and enjoy being together. When we trust our Father, we discover the freedom to celebrate life every day. We experience our worries being transformed into blessings.

Just like water being turned into wine.

CHAPTER FIVE

Like Little Children—He Always Had Time for the Kids

It must have been the roses and wine
Or maybe this unexplainable smile
They say where there's smoke there's fire
Well, I hope it's true
'Cause rumor has it, you love me too
—from "Rumor Has It"

Sometimes when I'm on the road, I miss my kids more than I can stand. If I'm gone for more than a couple days, I make sure I call them, text them, or Skype. When I first started out in the music business and my career began to take off, I would feel guilty if I was away from home too much. And then after my diagnosis of MS, I made a promise to myself to live with as few regrets as possible and changed my schedule when necessary to make sure I didn't miss out on watching my kids grow up.

I not only want to be there as my kids grow up, but I also want them to learn some of the same good old country values that I learned growing up. I'm convinced that kids who grow up in the country know what it's like to be raised with values that will last a lifetime. They know what it means to find joy in the simple things in life: making a nice catch down at the fishing hole, chasing lightning bugs at twilight on a summer evening and putting them in a Mason jar with holes in the lid to create a homemade flashlight.

Growing up country means doing chores and knowing that they had better be done right the first time. Mucking the stalls in the barn, milking the cows, feeding the chickens, slopping the pigs. Riding your bike into town, buying a Coke, putting peanuts in it, and watching the salt make it fizz—a lazy way of enjoying both treats at once. Getting your haircut at the barbershop—girls as well as boys. Going into the feed store, with its scent of hay, dog food, gasoline, and manure from somebody's boots.

I was fortunate enough to grow up in the country, and even though it wasn't easy, I wouldn't trade that childhood for anything. We were a few miles from the nearest paved road, and our closest neighbor was through the woods about a mile away. We grew our own vegetable garden, hunted for most of our meat, and got by on what we had. We learned to share and take care of one another. We learned that family always comes first and that you always love one another even if you don't always particularly like one another.

Jesus never married and didn't have any children. But he sure did love being around kids, and he always made time for them. In fact, he repeatedly valued children and encouraged us to be like them. "Then people brought little children to Jesus for him to place his hands on them and pray for them. But the disciples rebuked them. Jesus said, 'Let the little children come to me, and do not hinder them, for the kingdom of heaven belongs to such as these.' When he had placed his hands on them, he went on from there" (Matthew 19:13–15). This was one of my grandmother's favorite passages in the Bible, and she was constantly "letting the little children come" to her. She loved children as only a granny can and never turned away a child. She would babysit, share a meal, and invite kids to spend the night. Their youthful joy and sweet innocence was something she treasured.

By letting the little children come to him, and telling us to have our hearts and faith be like a child's, Jesus made it clear that kids are special.

As I think about what it means for us to be like little children, I think it's clear Jesus encourages us to be child*like* and not child*ish*. It's the difference between innocence and arrogance, alive with wonder versus spoiled and entitled. There are further clues in the Bible about what it means to be childlike, and they can strengthen our faith and remind us what being country is all about.

Go Fish

Like most kids, mine love to go to McDonald's. Now forgive me if it sounds irreverent, but every time I go there, I think of one of my favorite Bible stories, a miracle involving a bunch of hungry people and one little boy's lunch. It may seem like a big jump from a Filet-O-Fish sandwich to feeding more than five thousand people, but stick with me. I'm not sure they had American cheese and tartar sauce in Jesus's day, but they had plenty of bread and fish.

It's a simple meal, made out of what they had on hand, sort of like making a meal out of leftovers or putting together a casserole from what you have in the pantry. But at the heart of it, the miracle of the loaves and fishes came down to a few key ingredients: the needs of the people, Jesus's awareness of those needs, and the ability of the disciples to stretch their faith by exercising their imagination. Let's take a look.

*When Jesus landed and saw a large crowd, he had com-
passion on them, because they were like sheep without a
shepherd. So he began teaching them many things.*

*By this time it was late in the day, so his disciples
came to him. "This is a remote place," they said, "and
it's already very late. Send the people away so that they
can go to the surrounding countryside and villages and
buy themselves something to eat."*

But he answered, "You give them something to eat."

*They said to him, "That would take more than half
a year's wages! Are we to go and spend that much on
bread and give it to them to eat?"*

*"How many loaves do you have?" he asked. "Go
and see."*

When they found out, they said, "Five—and two fish."

*Then Jesus directed them to have all the people sit
down in groups on the green grass. So they sat down in
groups of hundreds and fifties. Taking the five loaves
and the two fish and looking up to heaven, he gave
thanks and broke the loaves. Then he gave them to his
disciples to distribute to the people. He also divided the
two fish among them all. They all ate and were satisfied, and the disciples picked up twelve basketfuls of
broken pieces of bread and fish. The number of the men
who had eaten was five thousand. (Mark 6:34–44)*

The feeding of the five thousand, as this spontaneous little picnic is usually called, is the only miracle described in all four of the New Testament Gospels. Which makes me think it must be especially important. It obviously had quite an impact on several thousand people and was one of the big public miracles that made quite a splash. But it also says a lot about the nature and character of God that he was willing to notice a very simple, basic need and then meet it. You don't have to be a kid to realize that Jesus cares about empty bellies and broken hearts. He fills our stomachs and heals our souls.

And the catalyst for this event, other than the physical need of the crowds, was one little boy's lunch. After Jesus has decided that they're responsible for feeding the multitudes, He sends the disciples out to see what they have to work with. They come back and say, "Here is a boy with five small barley loaves and two small fish, but how far will they go among so many?" (John 6:9).

Maybe the little guy thought ahead and packed it himself. Or maybe his mom or dad took the food they had and sent it with him. But regardless, out of all these thousands of people there to hear Jesus, apparently all the disciples could find was this boy's lunch. Now I don't know how small those fish actually were, but even if that was an understatement and they were each eighteen inches long, they still wouldn't usually be enough to feed more than a family of four. And maybe it's just because my wife's dinner rolls are so delicious, but our kids seem to go through a dozen of them all by themselves. No, five little barley loaves and a couple of fish were not much to work with.

But like the mustard seed of faith we're told is enough to move a mountain (Matthew 17:20), these humble fixings became the ingredients for a miracle. It strikes me sort of like the way my grandmother would take whatever she had on hand—no matter what it was, a lot or a little—and make an incredible meal out of it whenever company came to visit. She could have a whole ham or a couple slices of lunch meat and turn either one into a feast fit for a king.

I think she must've known Jesus's secret. And I think it has to do with a few things we can learn from this little boy who donated his lunch. First, he demonstrates that you should use what you've got and trust that it will be enough. Be resourceful and be creative. Often we spend time trying to obtain what we think everyone expects or needs or wants from us. Most of the time, however, they want only what we've got, no matter how simple or humble or plain that may be. We have to risk giving of ourselves in a way that trusts that who we are and what we have is more than enough. We have to remember that God blesses the resources he's given us and can multiply them to meet as many needs as he sees fit.

Love the Leftovers

Jesus had his disciples shepherd the crowds into groups of fifty to a hundred people, family-style—probably relatives with relatives or based on proximity, whomever they happened to be elbowing at the time. I smile, imagining what the disciples must've been thinking as they were getting ready for this little dinner party: I know he's the Lord and everything, but really? He wants us all to get together and huddle around a little old helping of . . . what? Five pieces of bread and a couple of fish?

Jesus then blesses the meager lunch and has it dispersed among the groups. Talk about stretching a meal to feed everybody at the table! Not only did everyone have enough to eat, but the disciples collected *twelve* baskets of leftovers! This miracle is often called the feeding of the five thousand, but based on the custom of the time, only the men were included in this figure. Factoring in the women and children who also partook of the lunch means the crowd could easily have been twice that number—at least ten thousand people! And every last one of them got to eat his or her fill, and still there were leftovers. That's some kind of fish sandwich!

This story also reminds us that God knows our needs and wants us to come to him with what we have, no matter how meager or ordinary it may seem. He has compassion for us like the shepherd for his sheep. He anticipates our needs even before we do. Not only does he know we need emotional and physical healing, but he understands we often need just the basics. "Give us this day, our daily bread," Jesus later teaches us to pray in the model that's known as the Lord's Prayer (more about this in a moment). He wants our basic daily needs—including physical hunger—to remind us of our deeper, spiritual hunger for God. This is why fasting can be so effective. Our empty stomachs remind us of the emptiness inside us that only God can fill.

Jesus tried to make this connection for his disciples. He tried to get them to notice the practical needs of all these people around them. Yes, they needed healing in their bodies, but they also simply needed something to eat. They were literally hungry. While the disciples grasped this need, they viewed it as a problem. "We don't want a bunch of hungry, tired people on our hands—not in a crowd this size. Better send them away now before they really get cranky!"

But the Lord was thinking, We can't let them go away on an empty stomach. What have we got to work with? This was a significant moment for the disciples, and for us today. So often, God wants to use you and me to be a part of someone else's miracle. Simply to take time and notice others around us. What are their needs? What are they walking through? What do they require that we can help provide?

The disciples were tired, they were busy—they had a lot to do; but Jesus reminded them that the needs of people were much more important than anything on their to-do list. If you've ever been around kids, from toddlers to teens, you know that they let you know when they're hungry. Most of them let you know exactly what they need. Similarly, we matter so much to God that we can bring our needs before him and know that he's going to listen to us and meet our needs.

As we grow out of childhood, it's easy to become disappointed and angry when our needs don't get met the way we want them to be. As a result, we all go through seasons when we question if anyone notices our needs. Does anyone notice me? Does anyone notice what I am going through here? Does anybody notice that I could use a miracle? Does God care about my needs? Can he really meet all my needs? From the groceries for our next meal to the doctor's bills waiting in our mailbox, he knows all our needs.

Just as a parent would never let his child go hungry, God makes sure we have enough of what we need. A needful position is a perfect position for a miracle, for God to show up. Children are dependent on their parents and must rely on them for food, shelter, clothing, education, and, most important, for their sense of worth. We all want to be loved. No matter how old we get or how mature we become, our need—our pain, our circumstance, no matter what it is, how big or small—has a way of defining us. But we must never give up hope about having our needs met. God knows the needs of his children and loves to give us good things.

Father's Day

This past Father's Day, I was reminded once again just how blessed I am. We made pancakes and I received some artwork I'll treasure for the rest of my life. My wife and kids treated me like a king and helped me realize why being a father is so special. I get to love and be loved in ways that point me back to God. Parenting is a humbling, scary, wonderful adventure, and there's no way to do it without relying on God as our Father.

Sometimes our earthly father makes it hard to relate to God as our Daddy for whatever reasons. I'm fortunate in that my father loved me and helped me be a better man than I would otherwise have been without him. I learned so much from my father about what it means to be a man, a husband, and a father. He taught me how to drive a tractor and plant a garden. How to sharpen a pocket knife. How to hunt quail and deer. How to appreciate nature and the beauty of God's creation that can be found only in green fields and old oak trees, a rolling hillside or a gushing creek.

Although he was not an earthly father, Jesus nevertheless knew the importance of loving and learning from his Father. He knew what it meant to be a good Son and obey his Father even when he didn't necessarily want to. He trusted his Daddy without any reservations, and he taught us to trust our Heavenly Father the same way. And he taught us to do the same, to approach God and talk with him like he's our Daddy.

As I mentioned earlier, my mama was a good Assembly of God woman, and my daddy was a lapsed Catholic. I sporadically attended both churches growing up in Texas and found myself more interested in what they had in common than in their many differences. One of those key similarities was the Lord's Prayer. The wording was slightly different, but the message was loud and clear.

When I got older and began studying my Bible more regularly, I discovered that Jesus gave us this model of how to pray in response to his disciples' question, "How are we supposed to pray?" (Luke 11:1). Apparently, the good old boys following John the Baptist, Jesus's cousin who had baptized him, had been praying a particular way, so Jesus's disciples wanted their own special way to pray, too.

Even before the Christian Church was founded, people were already worried about which way to do something rather than just focusing on doing the thing itself. So many denominations split hairs over the small things that they lose sight of the big things that God clearly wants all of us to do.

Being the good country boy that he was, though, Jesus explained how to make sure we keep our eyes on what's most important instead of getting lost in the details of which words to use or how loud our voice gets. He told his disciples:

"This, then, is how you should pray:
'Our Father in heaven,
hallowed be your name,
your kingdom come,
your will be done, on earth as it is in heaven.
Give us today our daily bread.
And forgive us our debts, as we also have forgiven our debtors.
And lead us not into temptation, but deliver us from the evil one.'" (Matthew 6:9–13)

Seems to me there are two big ideas here, according to Jesus, when we pray. First, we're supposed to relate to God not just as our Father, but as our Daddy. Second, our Daddy can provide all we need, whether it's our next meal or protection from our enemies. Best of all, he forgives us when we screw up and loves us enough to help us start over. Even if that means starting over every day.

Let's look at this first big idea for a moment. I can't tell you how much my heart melts when I walk into our house at the end of the day and hear my kids squeal, *"Daddy! Daddy! Daddy's home!"* There's no sweeter sound on this earth! No matter what kind of day I've had, how tired I am, how stressed I am, or what's weighing on me, when I hear their voices and they run to hug my neck, I'm the happiest man alive. I love to pick up my kids and put them on my shoulders or take them outside to swing or just to sit with them and hear all about their day.

If you're a parent, then you know what I'm talking about. And the Bible tells us that if we, who are human and sinful, love our children and want to give them our full attention, then how much more does our Heavenly Father love us. This was a radical concept for the Jewish people listening who had been taught to approach God in a very abstract, impersonal, detached kind of way.

In many ways, this entire approach to prayer broke in

content and in form with what his Jewish listeners were used to. Jesus declared that instead of praying only at set times and on set days at the synagogue, and instead of using the ancient words of their ancestors and the prophets, people could now communicate with Yahweh, the Lord of All, the Creator, the Holy One. Not only could they talk to him, but they could call him "Daddy."

Think of it this way. Imagine that you have a question about filing your federal income tax. You go online to a government website and fill out a form with your question to be sent to the Internal Revenue Service. You're expecting that it will take a few days or even a week or two before you get a response, and that your response will probably be from someone you've never heard of who answers citizens' questions.

Now imagine that a couple hours after you've e-mailed your question to the IRS, your doorbell rings. You go to answer it and can't believe your eyes when you open the door. There stands the president of the United States, and he says, "Hello, I believe you have a question about filling out your tax forms? Let's see if I can help." Or better yet, what if your *father* showed up at your door and he just happened to be the president!

This analogy isn't perfect, but maybe it gives you some idea of the contrast Jesus provided to his listeners. Certainly God is much more powerful than the president or any earthly position or human being. But Jesus brought a radical message to us: we can pray directly to God because he loves us as our Father. We can ask him for what we need and know that he will take care of us. We can ask him to forgive us for falling short and he will. We can ask for practical things, like daily bread or a fish sandwich, and he will hear us.

Jesus told us all we have to do is ask:

"Ask and it will be given to you; seek and you will find; knock and the door will be opened to you. For everyone who asks receives; the one who seeks finds; and to the one who knocks, the door will be opened.

"Which of you, if your son asks for bread, will give him a stone? Or if he asks for a fish, will give him a snake? If you, then, though you are evil, know how to give good gifts to your children, how much more will your Father in heaven give good gifts to those who ask him! So in everything, do to others what you would have them do to you, for this sums up the Law and the Prophets. (Matthew 7:7–12)

When my kids ask me for a peanut butter and jelly sandwich, I don't give them gravel and hot sauce! As parents, we want to give our kids what they want, and sometimes as they get older and their requests more expensive, we do so even when we're not sure it's best for them. Jesus explained that if we who are imperfect human parents experience this desire to give our kids the best, then how much more intense and real is this desire in our perfect Heavenly Father.

When we approach God from a child's point of view, with a child's honesty, sincerity, and humility, then he honors our request and makes sure we have what we need. Now, I'm not talking about treating him like a genie in a bottle or a wish machine that grants us new cars, beach houses, and millions in the bank. Because as we also know from being parents, we can't always give our children what they ask for when we know that it will obviously harm them. If my daughter asks to play with rat poison and my son wants to play with matches, I'm not going to let them. No, God doesn't always give us what we want or what we think we want. He gives us what we really need, the basics—especially love.

Child's Play

My son is at that stage where he's starting to think about how things work and the relationship between one thing and another. The other night he asked me where stars came from, which led to a question about the planets, which led to a discussion of Genesis, creation, God, the Bible, and all kinds of other things. His constant refrain of "How come?" started to get annoying after I heard it for about the twentieth time, but it also made me laugh. I love the way his little mind works and the passion and curiosity he brings to new information. He reminds me to cultivate this same sense of wonder in my own life and not to take everything at face value. He reminds me of another key lesson we can learn from being childlike: a sense of wonder.

I often spot this sense of wonder in the people I encounter who are smack dab in the middle of doing something they truly love. Recently, I ran into a man who is an expert on farm tools. We had a long conversation, and I was fascinated by this guy's knowledge of everything from tractors to plows and from hoes to horseshoes.

While I love farming and enjoyed hearing about this expert's collection and his experiences finding the various pieces, what I loved most was his passion. He clearly loves the land and is happiest soaking up the beauty of God's creation. His dedication and enthusiasm made me want to learn all I can about how to preserve the land and the best farm tools and equipment to use in the process.

He reminds me of another friend of mine, a luthier (that

is, a craftsman of guitars and other artisan-made stringed instruments). The musical instruments he creates are works of art and play sweeter than you can imagine. Again, it's clear that this guy has spent years of his life studying different types of wood, the relationship between pieces of wood, and how to wet them, mold them, shape them, plane them, and then string them together to produce what I often take for granted—the sweet sound of a well-made guitar. You can hear the love of music and musical instruments in my friend's voice as he describes his latest project. He starts talking real fast and then has to run to grab the neck of the guitar to show off the inlaid pieces he's just added.

Shortly after my visit with my friend the luthier, I came home and found my two youngest kids, both preschool age at the time, finger painting. The floor was covered with an old plastic-coated tablecloth that we use for picnics. Big sheets of white butcher paper offered my son and daughter an enormous canvas, which they were starting to fill with all sorts of colors and images. My son was leaning toward what appeared to be tractors, race cars, and what he said was a farm. My daughter was swirling butterflies, birds, and puffy clouds against a purple-blue sky. They were both giggling and laughing, making a mess and having a wonderful time.

When they saw me, they called me over to look at their paintings. Then they began to explain each picture and to talk about the colors they liked. They asked me which ones I liked best and if I wanted to join them. And you know what? I did! Their excitement and enthusiasm, their innocent passion over creating art for the pure joy of it was contagious.

Later, when we were cleaning up the mess we'd made and proudly displaying the kids' pictures on the side of the fridge, I realized that their level of enjoyment and engagement was very similar to my two friends. Those guys had learned how to keep their curiosity alive and to pour their energies into the things they loved most, whether that be farming tools or musical instruments. I'd like to think that I have the same kind of childlike wonder and excitement when I write songs, play music, and share my music with others.

When was the last time you found yourself immersed in doing something you love so much that you lost track of time? Are you able to pursue what you love doing? What have you always wanted to do but never made the time to discover? I challenge you to cultivate the kid inside you and pursue what makes your heart skip a beat. It may be quilt making or songwriting, gardening or furniture making, bear hunting or beekeeping, but whatever it is, become a child again. Let your mind remain curious and your heart full of wonder.

Under the Table

Jesus not only loved children, but he had a heart for families. He clearly wanted them to experience God in a new way, as a loving Father. The way he related to God as Father and lived as his Son demonstrates the value placed on family from the beginning. The fact that God chose to bring salvation to the Earth through a family—Mary and Joseph— also reinforces this idea. Just as he created Adam from dust and Eve from Adam's rib, God could've put Jesus on the Earth instantly. Instead, he chose to allow his Son to be born into a family.

And all throughout his ministry, Jesus wanted his miracles to point people back to a God who loved them in radical, surprising, joyful ways. He made it clear that all of us are God's children, not just the Jews. None of us are worthy, and all of us have been adopted as his sons and daughters. In fact, in one of his miraculous healings, Jesus makes it clear that our faith is the only thing required.

While there are a number of instances in which Jesus healed children, one in particular stands out to me. It involves a situation early in his public ministry when a foreign woman, a Canaanite, had a desperate need involving her daughter and wouldn't take no for an answer. Take a look:

Leaving that place, Jesus withdrew to the region of Tyre and Sidon. A Canaanite woman from that vicinity came to him, crying out, "Lord, Son of David, have mercy on me! My daughter is demon-possessed and suffering terribly."

Jesus did not answer a word. So his disciples came to him and urged him, "Send her away, for she keeps crying out after us."

He answered, "I was sent only to the lost sheep of Israel."

The woman came and knelt before him. "Lord, help me!" she said.

He replied, "It is not right to take the children's bread and toss it to the dogs."

"Yes it is, Lord," she said. "Even the dogs eat the crumbs that fall from their master's table."

Then Jesus said to her, "Woman, you have great faith! Your request is granted." And her daughter was healed at that moment. (Matthew 15:21–28)

This woman was a Gentile, an outsider, a non-Jewish person who was looked down upon. Even Jesus's disciples seemed to view her as a nuisance and less than worthy of their Master's attention. They viewed her as a stray dog who wandered into the kitchen during suppertime. They had not grown accustomed, or fully realized, that the message of the Gospel, the gift of grace wrapped up in the love of God, was and is for all people—not just the Jews. Even Jesus tried to indicate that he needed to remain focused on helping God's people, the Children of Israel, first before he extended his message to everyone else.

But this woman persisted and did so with humility and strength. She said that even the crumbs from the table would be enough to heal her daughter if Jesus was willing. And he was so impressed with her diligence and the sheer strength of her faith that he granted her desire and instantly healed her daughter. There was no logical reason for this woman to believe that Jesus would treat her any differently than any of the other Jews she'd encountered. There was no logical reason to even hope that he could do what she had only heard through rumor and whispers and gossip from neighbors outside of Jerusalem. Could this man who claimed to be the Son of God really have the power to heal the anguish of her poor, tormented daughter?

This woman was so desperate she knew that she had nothing to lose and everything to gain. She had nowhere else to turn and knew that there had to be hope, there had to be a way for her child to be restored. A mother's love is fierce, and here we see a tenacity and a depth of love that should inspire us to trust God with our deepest needs. The disciples were still figuring things out; they couldn't help her and didn't particularly want Jesus to help her. Only the Lord himself could help this woman. He recognized the intensity of her faith and granted her request.

In all his encounters and references to children, Jesus makes it clear that we have a lot to learn from them. He said we must enter God's kingdom with the heart of a child. He relied on a boy's lunch to perform one of the largest miracles of his time on Earth. He taught us how to pray from the posture of a child talking to his Daddy. Time and time again, he emphasized the importance of families. And through all of these experiences, he showed us how our faith can carry us through even when we feel like we're at the end of our rope. Yes, Jesus was a country boy, but he also knew what it was like to be a kid at heart.

CHAPTER SIX

Expect the Unexpected—
He Loved to Surprise

Growing up under that hometown church steeple
Learning God hates sin but still loves people
The preacher preaching 'bout the Promised Land
And me thinking 'bout holding Jesse Lane's hand

And one hot summer when I was thirteen
Took my soul to the river and washed it clean
Feels so good, Lord, why can't there be
Seven Sundays a week?

—FROM "SEVEN SUNDAYS"

One of the things I love best about performing for my audiences is the thrill of surprising them. When I was just starting out, I learned that there has to be a balance between giving a crowd what they want or expect out of a show and surprising them with more than they expected. It might be a cover of a song that they'd never expect me to do, like a pop hit or a mushy love song. It might be adding certain songs from my playlist and giving others a rest. It might be giving them an encore that they'll never forget.

Sometimes I'll have the opportunity to invite a well-known friend to join a set as a special guest star. I've been fortunate in getting to meet and perform with some of my idols, people like George Jones, Loretta Lynn, Reba McEntire, and George Strait. They're all class acts and are just as warm and down-to-earth as you'd imagine.

Along the way, I've also met a number of celebrities—musicians, performers, movie stars, and public figures—who weren't quite so friendly and comfortable around other people. These are the ones who always surprise me, because it's clear that what they present to the public is not really who they are the rest of the time. They're more concerned with image, good press, and a positive marketing spin than with who they are inside.

And audiences go wild when they realize that something wonderful and unexpected has just been given to them. They were already having a good time, and suddenly they can't believe that they're getting to see something spontaneous and special, something unique that's just for them. A different set list. A new song I've written that's never been performed in front of an audience before. A duet with a country superstar whom they love as much as I do. All of a sudden their expectations have been exceeded, and it has nothing to do with anything they've done to make it happen. It's like finding a twenty-dollar bill in the pocket of an old pair of jeans or receiving a gift in the mail from someone you haven't heard from in a while.

I think as we grow up and become adults, we lose that childlike sense of enjoying surprises. We discover that there are some unpleasant ones and begin to forget that there are still great things coming our way. But God delights in surprising his children. A red sunset lighting up the evening sky, the taste of a fresh homegrown tomato, having a friend drop by for no reason other than to sit on the front porch with a glass of sweet tea and shoot the breeze. He also delights in surprising us with big things—miraculous news back from your doctor, an unexpected windfall that's the exact amount of your car repairs, getting a job you love after being laid off. And of course, the biggest surprise of all—the gift of his Son.

What It's All About

It's clear from his various encounters with a wide variety of people that Jesus also surprised most of them. Some were likely overjoyed to discover that he was the Messiah, the Son of God with the power to forgive them, heal them, love them like no one ever had. Others, however, were disappointed that he wasn't focused on military power, monetary wealth, or personal achievements.

In fact, right from the moment he arrived on the scene, Jesus never conformed to the expectations of the majority. It's almost as if God deliberately wanted to make his point over and over again. Power on this earth is not what it's all about. Love, forgiveness, and grace are what's it's all about. Being religious and following a bunch of rules and imposing them on other people is not what it's about. Loving God in a direct, personal relationship is what it's all about.

But after waiting hundreds of years for the birth of the long-prophesied Messiah, the Son of God, the Jewish people developed certain expectations. They assumed that since God was all powerful, all knowing, and all loving that he would reveal his Son in a way that conformed to earthly assumptions. Namely, that the Messiah would hold a royal pedigree, would be born in a palace, would assume the throne, and would lead a big army.

As we all know, this scenario couldn't have been further from who Jesus was and how he lived. And it all started with the way he came into the world. Not as a royal heir in a warm, elaborate palace where his every need would be met, but as a baby in a manger, huddled there in a cow shed beneath the stars.

The Reason for the Season

Christmastime always gets me going. Maybe it's just the kid in me, but I love the anticipation, the excitement in the air, the scent of evergreen from a fresh-cut tree, the way the lights glisten through a frost-kissed window. I love the songs and the carols, the way people seem to take a little more time to spend with those they love the most. I love the way the kids laugh and giggle, adding to their wish lists, dreaming of more toys than they can possibly play with. Most of all, I love buying presents.

Now I confess that I'm not a big shopper. I'm much more likely to order something online or to go with something I stumble across while I'm traveling. But I love the feeling of finding a unique necklace that I know will bring a smile to Jessie's beautiful face. Or discovering a telescope that will light up my little boy's expression more than the stars light up the night sky. Or a teddy bear made from old quilts and fabric scraps that my youngest daughter will name and hold in her arms at bedtime.

I wasn't always this way, of course. As a kid, it was all about what I wanted and hoped Santa Claus would bring me. We didn't have much, but my parents always seemed to find a way to get me something I wanted—a new bike, a racetrack, a boom box with cassettes of my favorite artists, and, one year, a new guitar. But once I grew up and became a father, I soon learned that I wasn't as excited about what I received.

Sure, I like getting presents as much as anyone does, but I usually wasn't going to be very surprised. The real joy, I discovered, came from seeing my kids' eyes light up as they came downstairs on Christmas morning. Watching their smiles bloom from a hopeful grin to an ear-to-ear smile as they opened a present. Listening to them squeal with sheer joy as they unwrapped the toy that they had only dared to hope might be under the tree.

Sometimes I wonder if this is the same kind of experience God has as our Father. I mean, originally, he created people, human beings beginning with Adam and Eve, so that he could have a relationship with us. I don't know that he ever got lonely, but he sure did seem to enjoy walking with our original great-great-great-grandparents in the cool of the garden. Maybe like any new parent, he was beside himself with joy just to interact with these new beings created in his image.

But then they let him down—let all of us down—by choosing to disobey God and eat the fruit from the forbidden tree. They sinned, a word that may sound old-fashioned to us but that simply means they missed the mark. They messed up. And as a result, they lost the incredible gift of fellowship with God that they had taken for granted up until then.

So God had to go about finding another way to gift his children with his presence (and with his presents). After many hundreds of years and dozens of generations, his plan culminated in the birth of his Son, Jesus. Now as spectacular and history making and life changing as this event was, it happened in the most nonspectacular, unglamorous, unexpected way possible. It was going to be a surprise present like no other before or since.

The Greatest Gift

First of all, it started with a very unsuspecting young woman, a young teenager named Mary. Engaged to an upstanding, hardworking carpenter from Nazareth, Mary assumed they would enjoy a quiet, low-key, pleasant life together. They were both honest, God-fearing, people-loving kind of folks, and each was happy with the match. And then faster than you can say "Surprise!" an angel pops in on Mary with an announcement that changed everything.

> *"Greetings, you who are highly favored! The Lord is with you."*
>
> *Mary was greatly troubled at his words and wondered what kind of greeting this might be. But the angel said to her, "Do not be afraid, Mary; you have found favor with God. You will conceive and give birth to a son, and you are to call him Jesus. He will be great and will be called the Son of the Most High. The Lord God will give him the throne of his father David, and he will reign over Jacob's descendants forever; his kingdom will never end."*
>
> *"How will this be," Mary asked the angel, "since I am a virgin?"*
>
> *The angel answered, "The Holy Spirit will come on you, and the power of the Most High will overshadow you. So the holy one to be born will be called the Son of God." (Luke 1:28–35)*

Not what she expected to hear in the middle of her day. And then when the angel tells her why he's come, she asks a very logical, although slightly awkward question. Can't you just imagine this shy, reserved, humble young woman wondering, "Uh, excuse me, but I mean, well, what do you mean exactly? How can I have God's Son if I've never, uh, you know, done what it takes to become with child?"

And the angel's response was direct and straightforward—basically, that God will take care of it. That his Holy Spirit would overshadow her and cause her to conceive this Child by the power of God. I love that term, "overshadow," because it reminds us that God's authority, wisdom, knowledge, and goodness are greater than all of us. He constantly overshadows us, and when we resist him, then we end up missing out on the extraordinary gifts he wants to give us.

Mary accepted the news with remarkable grace, as befitting the woman chosen by God to be the mother of his Son. A few months later, when she visits her cousin Elizabeth, who was also with child, a baby boy who would grow up to be John the Baptist, Mary shares a prayer known as the Canticle of Mary, or the Magnificat, that conveys about the best response to God's surprises that I've ever found.

And Mary said: "My soul proclaims the greatness of the Lord and my spirit rejoices in God my Saviour; because he has looked upon the humiliation of his servant. Yes,

from now onwards all generations will call me blessed,
for the Almighty has done great things for me. Holy
is his name, and his faithful love extends age after age
to those who fear him. He has used the power of his
arm, he has routed the arrogant heart. He has pulled
down princes from their thrones and raised high the
lowly. He has filled the starving with good things, sent
the rich away empty. He has come to the help of Israel
his servant, mindful of his faithful love—according to
the promise he made to our ancestors—of his mercy
to Abraham and to his descendants forever." (Luke
1:46–55, NJB)

Joseph also had to deal with this supernatural surprise,
and I'm guessing, for him, it wasn't quite so pleasant at
first. Here's the woman he loves, a gal who's simple, sweet,
honest, innocent, and pure, and all of a sudden she tells him
that she's pregnant—by God. Wow, talk about having a
bombshell dropped on you by the one you love! He obviously knew that he was not the father of this baby growing
inside his fiancée. And had the dear woman gone crazy?
Could it really be possible that this child was from God? Or
had something terrible happened that she just couldn't bear
to tell him?

Regardless of what he was thinking, Joseph displayed a strength and integrity of character that few men can muster. Initially, he decided to have her put away quietly and not embarrass her (Matthew 1:19). If he wanted to avoid the rumors and nasty gossip that were bound to spring up, Joe could easily have made a spectacle of poor Mary and tried to distance himself from her and her situation. Ironically enough, much like the religious leaders who attempted to condemn the woman caught in adultery when they brought her before Jesus, Joseph could've acted self-righteous and condescending. Instead, he received a special message from an angel himself.

But after he had considered this, an angel of the Lord appeared to him in a dream and said, "Joseph, son of David, do not be afraid to take Mary home as your wife, because what is conceived in her is from the Holy Spirit. She will give birth to a son, and you are to give him the name Jesus, because he will save his people from their sins."

When Joseph woke up, he did what the angel of the Lord had commanded him and took Mary home as his wife. But he did not consummate their marriage until she gave birth to a son. And he gave him the name Jesus. (Matthew 1:20–21, 24–25)

Good News

From that moment on, the birth of Jesus continued to surprise everyone aware of his arrival. Instead of being born in a comfortable home in Jerusalem surrounded by family and friends, he is born in a back-road village that's probably not much bigger than the town where I grew up. We know that it was small because when the Romans decided to take a census and have everyone return to the place from which their ancestors originated, there was no room in any of the usual places to stay. It probably had only one inn, and that inn probably filled up fast with the people who arrived first and could afford it.

Our humble newlyweds, however, ended up out in the fields, not far from the shepherds, I'm guessing, under the stars. With only a few barnyard friends to keep them company, they prepared for the imminent arrival of God's Son. As the cries of their newborn filled their ears, Mary wrapped her baby boy in strips of cloth, "swaddling clothes," that would keep him snug and warm.

Their first visitors weren't dignitaries, royalty, and world religious leaders. No, the first people to receive the news about the Messiah's birth were just good old boys out in the fields tending their flocks by night. Once again, an angel caught them by surprise with the most amazing and unsettling news they'd ever heard. "Do not be afraid.

I bring you good news that will cause great joy for all the people. Today in the town of David a Savior has been born to you; he is the Messiah, the Lord" (Luke 2:10–11). Just to make their point even clearer, the angels provide a free concert to express their joy.

Yes, the three kings from the East show up later, but I think it's significant that the first people to learn the news are everyday joes, working men out doing their job. And when the foreign VIPs do show up, they had to work to find the new infant king. When they went to King Herod and asked, he freaked out and subsequently had all the baby boys in the area killed because he assumed that the new king would be a traditional, conventional royal who would someday want to take the throne. No one seemed to realize that the Kingdom Jesus came to rule was much larger than Palestine, or the Roman Empire, or even the world. Ultimately, he came to rule the kingdom within us, the kingdom of the human heart.

Word Made Flesh

With his humble birth that surprised everyone waiting on the Messiah, Jesus became the living proof, "God with us," that God loves us enough to send the most precious gift he had. Our Creator wanted to have a relationship with us so much that he was willing to send his only Son to this crazy, wonderful, messed-up world.

And it wasn't just his birth that clearly upended Jewish expectations for their Messiah. Everything he did throughout his public ministry, from mingling with tax collectors and prostitutes to healing lepers and feeding thousands, never conformed to what those in power might have wanted. They expected a powerful—at least by earthly standards—king who would use divine military might to restore their nation to supremacy as God's chosen nation. What they got was a king, powerful beyond earthly imaginations, who would use his divine might to serve the desperate, downtrodden, and despondent.

Christ made it explicitly clear that the kingdom he was ushering in was eternal and not temporal, heavenly and not earthly, spiritual and not physical. While those around him, including his own disciples, often clamored for him to seize governmental control, he made it clear that earthly power was not his goal. Just after Jesus was arrested in the Garden of Gethsemane, after he had been interrogated by the high priest, Caiaphas, he was brought before Pontius Pilate, the Emperor Caesar's designated governor over the Jewish territory then occupied by Rome.

Pilate wasted no time with his unusual Jewish prisoner

and asked point-blank: "Are you the king of the Jews?" (John 18:33). Basically, he assumed that the direct approach would be the most telling. Today it would be like going before your state governor and having him or her ask you, "Do you really think you're the president?"

In his typical way of surprising people, Jesus did not defend himself, choosing neither to refute nor verify Pilate's inquiry. Instead, he returned the Roman governor's question with one of his own.

"Is that your own idea," Jesus asked, "or did others talk to you about me?"

"Am I a Jew?" Pilate replied. "Your own people and chief priests handed you over to me. What is it you have done?"

Jesus said, "My kingdom is not of this world. If it were, my servants would fight to prevent my arrest by the Jewish leaders. But now my kingdom is from another place."

"You are a king, then!" said Pilate.

Jesus answered, "You say that I am a king. In fact, the reason I was born and came into the world is to testify to the truth. Everyone on the side of truth listens to me."

"What is truth?" retorted Pilate. (John 18:34–38)

King of the Hill

This interrogation was most unusual, and perhaps even confusing, for the Roman governor. His straightforward question—"Are you the king of the Jews?"—was probably expected to produce or yes or no response from the prisoner. It was a simple, logical question that should have had a clear, unequivocal answer. Either you are a king of some sort—either Jewish royalty or someone claiming authority through military support—which means you're a threat to Roman occupation, or you're not, which means you're just another citizen who's causing trouble. Yes or no, are you a king?

But as was typical, Jesus didn't give the expected response. Instead, he explained that his kingdom was "not of this world," which does indeed imply that he is a king of some kind. Kingdoms are ruled by kings, right? However, the categories held at that time, by Pilate as well as the Jews, were concrete, geographical, and nationalistic. How could one have a kingdom that was *not* a worldly kingdom? Jesus's response must have seemed a little crazy to the Roman leader, who obviously hadn't risen to his position of power by talking in riddles and clever metaphors.

No, political and military leaders at the time held a worldview that persists to this day. This King of the Hill mind-set is at its core fundamentally competitive, controlling, and power-based. It's like the kids' game that I enjoyed as a boy on the playground at school. We'd divide up into teams, establish a boundary line between us, and create a home base to claim, the "hill," or a flag to capture in between.

This King of the Hill paradigm evolved quite naturally in a world where individuals wanted what they wanted and believed they could take it by force. Whoever had the most—the most soldiers, the largest army, the craftiest generals, the most powerful weapons, the most advanced technology—won. This winner-take-all system certainly prevailed for the nation of Israel up until Jesus's time. Sorely outnumbered, they had to trust God with the impossible odds of conquering the Canaanites in order to enter the Promised Land. From then on, it was a constant tug-of-war struggle to fend off invading tribes and nations and hold on to what God had given them or to try to claim more.

So with this very human idea of power in mind, it's no wonder that the people of Jesus's day expected him to be a popular, power-wielding, royal-tyrant-style leader. His disciples would even get into squabbles over who would get to sit closest to him once he was ruling. They assumed that once he had built his grassroots foundation based on popular appeal, he would do what any other man would do—grab control of the national reins and guide them in his direction.

When he didn't pursue political control, it only served to confuse everyone. Perhaps none were more disappointed and confused than his followers when he was finally put to death on a cross like a common criminal. Their Master had done nothing illegal or unethical and had only helped those who wanted to be helped. And yet, he refused to fight back, to defend himself, to resist arrest when Judas betrayed him and the resentful religious leaders came for him.

And then to see their beloved friend and leader, the One they were convinced was indeed the Son of God, tortured and mocked must've been unbearable. Maybe they kept wondering how long Jesus would allow this kind of abuse and perversion of justice to continue. Maybe they thought that he was going to let it go up to the very last second before he called in a host of angels with some lightning bolts to clear the scene. But he didn't. Jesus allowed the Jewish people to drive pieces of iron through his hands and feet and fasten him to a couple pieces of wood stuck in the ground on a barren hillside.

When the Lord took his last mortal breath, those around him must've wondered what happened. How had they allowed themselves to believe that this guy could really be the Messiah? Surely, if he had been, then he would never have allowed the unthinkable to happen. If he were really God's Son, then he would not have allowed himself to be put to death.

Would he?

Seeing Is Believing

While it must have been an incredibly depressing and bleak couple of days, Jesus had the surprise of all surprises left to spring. He might have died on the cross, but the story was far from over. In fact, the story didn't end there—it actually began there. When some of the women came to his tomb early the morning of the third day, they discovered the ultimate disappearing trick. Jesus wasn't there! The two-ton stone had been rolled back and the gravesite was empty. I'll bet none of them had dared hope for such a miraculous moment.

His disciples . . . well, they needed some convincing. Jesus walked with some of them along the road to Emmaus and then met all of them in the upper room, a place in which they had locked themselves. And then suddenly, once again, surprise! Their Lord was standing there in their midst.

And you have to love good old doubting Thomas. This guy had the guts to say what we might have all felt at one time or another. "Unless I see the scars from the nail holes in his hands and place my fingers into his side where the spear pierced him, then I can't believe it's really my Lord." But then when given the chance, Thomas knows beyond a shadow of a doubt that Jesus was alive and standing in front of Him. Jesus said, "Blessed are those who have not seen and still believe" (John 20:29).

The resurrection is at the heart of our Christian faith. It sounds crazy, impossible, unbelievable. And yet, it's true. There was a much bigger goal in place than just trying to restore the nation of Israel to its former glory. Jesus came to set all of us free, not just a few, not just the ones who were there at the time or had come before him. His gift keeps on giving because he brings all of us the gift of grace and for-giveness for all of time.

Mugged in Music City

Maybe it's the fact that Jesus was such a rebel, such a non-conformist with the religious bigwigs of his day that makes me question the way we often relate to one another today, in the twenty-first century. Too often, it seems as if the church is often about excluding certain people instead of including everyone. People claiming to be Christians picket, protest, and boycott anything that they think doesn't fit their way of doing things. They hide behind the Bible and shout a one-way conversation instead of trying to have a conversation that reveals the love of God.

I was reminded of this again recently when a friend of mine, Mike, came to town with his family. He and his wife were facing a major milestone since their oldest daughter was getting married, the first of their children to leave the nest for good. His daughter had met a good old southern boy here in Nashville and had fallen in love. Mike and his family, who live in Colorado, were tickled as pigs in mud when they learned they were going to have a Tennessean in the family.

As the nuptials approached, I was excited to learn that Mike was coming to town for his soon-to-be new son-in-law's bachelor party. He and I made plans to get together for dinner before he left since he and two of his sons, along with several other out-of-town buddies of the groom, were staying at a nice hotel in downtown Nashville. Knowing what big hockey fans they are, I encouraged them to take in a hockey game that Saturday night, one that seemed perfect for the bride and groom: the Nashville Predators versus the Colorado Avalanche!

After checking in on Friday night, Mike and the guys strolled down Broadway a few blocks from their hotel toward a local restaurant and bar that featured live country and bluegrass music. They figured that since they were in Music City they ought to experience country music firsthand, and this place came highly recommended from multiple sources, myself included. Along the way, they passed numerous other bars and restaurants, along with a strip club, a pawnshop, a convenience store, and a couple of tattoo parlors. Not necessarily the nicest part of the city, but certainly not a dangerous or crime-ridden area.

Just as they reached the block where their restaurant was located, they noticed a commotion across the street where a handful of people were holding up signs and shouting in unison. Curious at what was going on, as Mike and the bachelor party got closer, they read signs proclaiming, REPENT OR BURN, WAGES OF SIN IS DEATH—AND YOU'RE WORKING OVERTIME, and HELL IS REAL. The small group of evangelists shouted out similar messages along with assorted Bible verses.

Now Mike and his family are strong Christians, but he knew that some of the groom's friends were not. As they got closer to their destination, the ten guys in the bachelor party became the focus of the street preachers. While the young men tried to ignore the angry noise, Mike smiled and waved, unafraid to acknowledge his faith and hoping to salvage the non-Christians' impressions. In fact, my buddy Mike decided to go over and talk with the dozen men and women who were obviously so passionate about their faith.

Mike soon realized, however, after attempting to engage this little group for several minutes, that they weren't about to believe that he was a Christian. One of them even said, "Sir, if you were a *true* Christian, you would not be entering an establishment dedicated to alcohol and immorality." These guys obviously didn't know my friend Mike, because to him these were fighting words.

He responded, "Sir, if *you* were a true Christian, you'd be serving dinner down at the rescue mission instead of making assumptions and heckling tourists. It's easy to judge someone by their appearance or location, but it takes holy humility to serve those in need." He then turned and walked away, hearing one of the group call out after him, "We'll pray for your salvation!" to which Mike responded, "And I'll pray for yours."

Mike shared this incident with me when we had dinner together the following night, and he was quick to acknowledge that he hadn't necessarily handled the situation well. "It just makes me so angry, Clay," he said. "Did those folks really think that somebody was going to walk up to them and say, 'Oh, I didn't realize that I was doing anything wrong until I saw your sign! Please tell me what I need to do so I can be a good Christian just like you!'" As he continued, Mike explained what a disappointment it had been. "One of the groom's friends said he felt as if he'd been mugged! And truth be told, I guess I did, too," Mike said. "Tell me that this is not what Nashville is like!"

After I'd made it clear that Nashville was one of the finest cities in the world, with some of the nicest, kindest, most hospitable people of every faith persuasion, Mike told me, "Don't get me wrong—I'm not against street evangelism or making an outpost in enemy territory. I just wonder if those guys we encountered were there for the benefit of others, or just for themselves."

Mike's experience left me unsettled, and I wondered how I would've handled the situation myself. Because I'm often recognized when I'm out in public, I try to be deliberate about being approachable, friendly, and down-to-earth. But with these street evangelists whom Mike encountered, I'm afraid I would've lost it. If nothing else, I would like to have reminded them that Jesus wasn't afraid to risk his reputation in order to love everyone—sinners, prostitutes, lepers, and tax collectors included.

At a deeper level, I found Mike's final comment very thought provoking. How often do we do things in the name of Jesus so that we can feel better about ourselves and prove that we're "really Christians" instead of doing them with humility and compassion for the true benefit of those around us? I don't want to judge the handful of evangelists whom Mike and his guys encountered in Nashville. For one, I wasn't there, and secondly, I know that street preaching can certainly be something that God uses to draw people to him. However, the fact that someone felt "spiritually mugged" just for walking past them says a lot.

Love Like You Mean It

Instead of judging others, I believe Jesus invites us to treat others with extra kindness and compassion. It's easy to condemn someone so that you can feel better about yourself. But acknowledging that we're all human, all in need of the grace Jesus came to give us, keeps us honest, humble, and dependent on God. We don't have to have all the answers when we keep our eyes on the only perfect Country Boy who ever lived.

With the example of Jesus in mind, I'm convinced we're called to live our lives out of the box, with wonder and joy and a sense of the unexpected. We need to keep our eyes open for opportunities to get off the rat-race treadmill and discover the small moments that make life worth living. We need to look for opportunities to surprise others with the gifts of our time, our presence, our resources. So much of life these days seems to be about doing what other people expect us to do. If we based our knowledge of people on Facebook, we would have to assume that everyone is enjoying a perfect life with exotic vacations, expensive toys, and homes in exclusive neighborhoods.

Jesus invites us to be rebels, not to be like the people more in love with religion than with God. He set the standard for what it means to be true to our Father's direction and not the expectations of religious people around us. His entire life upended the expectations of those around him. From his humble origins in a manger to his crucifixion like a common criminal, Jesus made it clear that power is not about wealth, political clout, or manipulation. It's about being true to your real identity.

Country boys and country gals know their roots, and their fruits show it. Jesus said, "By this everyone will know that you are my disciples, if you love one another" (John 13:35). When we follow the One who still challenges us to redefine power and reassess how we live our lives, we discover a fresh perspective. It doesn't matter which church we go to or how many times we attended last month. All we have to do is remain open to the gifts that God wants to give us. All we have to do is love like we mean it.

Jesus Knew How to LOVE

★

CHAPTER SEVEN

The Least of These—He Had Friends in Low Places

Heaven help the fool who did her wrong
It's too late, too bad, she's too far gone
He should have thought of that
Before he left her all alone
If she's lonely now, she won't be lonely long

—FROM "SHE WON'T BE LONELY LONG"

Love songs appear in virtually every kind of music known: classical, jazz, rock, opera, pop, and even Gospel. And while I'm biased, I don't think any musical genre relies on love as much as country music does. The songs basically fall into two categories—falling in love and falling out of love—and I'm not sure which is more powerful. Just think about timeless songs like Patsy Cline's "Crazy," or Conway

Twitty's "Hello, Darlin'." Songs like "I Walk the Line" and "Gentle on My Mind," "Feels So Right" and "Forever and Ever, Amen," not to mention more contemporary classics like Dolly Parton's "I Will Always Love You" and Faith Hill's "Breathe."

I suspect, though, that the sad songs might outnumber the feel-good, mushy love songs in country music. A veteran songwriter once told me that you can't write a good country song unless there's whiskey, cheating, or kissing involved, and if you can get all three in, then it's bound to be a hit! Seriously, the heartache expressed by the immortal "I'm So Lonesome I Could Cry" or "He Stopped Loving Her Today" makes all of us feel the intense pain that occurs when we've lost someone we love. And what would country music be without songs like Miss Reba's "For My Broken Heart" or Vince Gill's "When I Call Your Name"?

Regardless of the type of song you prefer, I suspect that we couldn't have one without the other. We wouldn't experience such pain and loneliness over what we've lost if it hadn't felt so wonderful in the beginning. And over the course of our lifetime, most of us have been on both sides of those relationships. Maybe that's why love is such a powerful force and timeless theme in all kinds of music.

But music isn't the only way to express feelings about what it means to love someone. If you consider all the advice, input, and information about love we receive from how-to books, romance novels, reality TV shows, movies, and online dating services, then you'd assume no one would ever be by themselves again. Despite the overload of information about love, however, we often miss the true meaning of what it is to love someone. Once again, in order to remind ourselves of the truth, it's a good idea to look at the Good Book to see the example Jesus set.

Pay Your Taxes

As we've seen, Jesus came to shake things up and change history once and for all. But he wasn't just the ultimate Country Boy fighting for his Father's kingdom. No matter what he was doing or whom he encountered, Jesus was always motivated by love. Not the romantic love we often hear so much about in our popular culture, but a divine, selfless, God-inspired love that's at the core of who we are and who he is. And perhaps this kind of love is most apparent in the way that Jesus loved the people whom no one else loved, the outsiders and outcasts, the weak and the wounded, the poor and the powerless.

Even the guys he chose to be his closest friends, the disciples, weren't the cream of the crop, elite members of society.

They were just regular, hardworking, no-nonsense kind of people—fishermen and tax collectors. Earlier in this book, we looked at Jesus's encounter with the tax collector Zacchaeus, but long before he called out to the little man in the sycamore tree, Christ had already gotten to know another tax man, Levi, or as he came to be called, Matthew.

After this, Jesus went out and saw a tax collector by the name of Levi [also known as Matthew] sitting at his tax booth. "Follow me," Jesus said to him, and Levi got up, left everything and followed him.

Then Levi held a great banquet for Jesus at his house, and a large crowd of tax collectors and others were eating with them. But the Pharisees and the teachers of the law who belonged to their sect complained to his disciples, "Why do you eat and drink with tax collectors and sinners?"

Jesus answered them, "It is not the healthy who need a doctor, but the sick. I have not come to call the righteous, but sinners to repentance." (Luke 5:27–32)

Now tax collectors were about as welcome in the local community as foxes in a hen house. Working for the Roman government occupying Israel, these tax men would collect the amount required by Caesar and then as much above that percentage as possible, which they would keep for themselves. For all we know, Levi, or Matthew, may have been the wealthiest of the men whom Jesus called to be a disciple. The fact that he threw a huge banquet at his house in honor of Jesus would reinforce this notion. Interestingly enough, his friends in attendance were mostly tax collectors themselves.

And there's also little doubt that good old Matt was an outsider from the self-righteous religious leaders, who immediately started wagging their tongues and criticizing Jesus for hanging in Mattie's hood. Even the fact that Jesus asked Matthew in the first place seems significant and reminds us that he didn't care what other people might think. He was interested in what's inside a person, not in what they look like, the kind of profession they had, or what their reputation was. I'm guessing Jesus's invitation may have caught Levi by surprise since he wasn't usually at the top of people's guest lists.

All the more reason to throw a party and tell the friends he did have about this new guy, Jesus, who was so accepting and warm, so appealing and genuinely caring. It reminds us that when we experience unconditional acceptance and love, we naturally want to share it with those around us. Matthew had met someone who was radically changing his life, and he wanted his friends to experience the same thing. Can't you just imagine his excitement? "Come on over! You have to meet this guy who's rocking my world! In fact, I'm quitting my job so I can follow him!"

When the religious leaders complained about the kind of company Jesus was keeping, he didn't mince words in his response to them: "Hey, I'm here to help the sick, not the ones who think they're healthy. I'm looking for people who know they need more in their lives, not the ones who think they have it all together." His words probably only outraged these uptight religious snobs even more. They couldn't grasp why someone claiming to be the Son of God would ever allow himself to be among the lowest of the low. But that was Jesus's point—and they missed it.

Drinking with a Shady Lady

It wasn't just tax collectors like Zacchaeus and Matthew whom Jesus sought out and hung with. He interacted with and impacted numerous women as well. In fact, one of the things I love most about the example Jesus set for us is the way he treated women: with respect, kindness, compassion, and dignity.

First off, remember the culture during his lifetime. Many men owned women, either as slaves or through the legalities of marriage. And of course, polygamy was accepted and even expected, so no man had to depend on any one woman for anything—not love, not sex, not children, nothing. If a woman was quiet, submissive, only married to one man and able to provide him with sons, then she would be considered adequate—not praiseworthy or exceptional, mind you—just adequate.

Knowing this makes Jesus's encounters with various women all the more startling. One in particular has always intrigued me, a conversation with a woman whom I refer to as "a shady lady" for reasons that will soon become apparent. This woman was a Samaritan who must've certainly had her share of looks, whispers, catty remarks, and catcalls as she walked by on her way to collect water at the well. In fact, it was around noon—the hottest part of the day, when few people dared to brave the scorching sun—when she met a foreign man, a Jew, there at the public well.

When he asked her for a drink, she reminded him that she was a Samaritan and he was a Jew and, well, it wasn't socially acceptable. Maybe for us today, it would have been like an African American man asking a white woman for a drink during the civil rights movement of the 1960s. Well-meaning people who didn't want to cause trouble avoided such encounters—you just didn't go there.

But just as he wasn't influenced by the judgmental crowd buzzing about his presence at Matthew's dinner party, Jesus wasn't fazed by the social standards of the day, particularly ones based on prejudice. So he kept talking to her, drawing her out—not so much for his benefit as for hers.

Through their surprising conversation, this woman learns that Jesus is no ordinary traveler passing through and asking for a drink. He not only knows about local customs—he knows that she's had five husbands and that she's not even married to her current live-in. Greater still—and this is what's truly astounding—he knows that she longs for more than any husband or romantic relationship can ever provide.

He knows that her heart is parched for what he calls "living water," the mercy and grace, forgiveness and cleansing that only God can pour out. As Jesus explains to her, "Everyone who drinks this water will be thirsty again, but whoever drinks the water I give them will never thirst. Indeed, the water I give them will become in them a spring of water welling up to eternal life" (John 4:13–14).

Once again, the Master makes it clear that he didn't come to earth to set up a country club and admit an elite few. He came to meet a basic human need—spiritual thirst—in all people who are willing to drink from his heavenly well. He came to treat those who are sick, those in need, those people who aren't satisfied playing the religious game—including women.

The Sweet Smell of Success

Now Jesus wasn't a "ladies' man" in the way we tend to use that phrase, but he certainly respected and defended women like the true Country Boy he was. From the time we're knee-high to a grasshopper, as my daddy used to say, country boys are taught to treat females with courtesy, kindness, and respect. It's not that women are weak and fragile and have to be treated like they're made of glass. It's simply a way to acknowledge the differences in the way God made men and women. Both are made in his image, we're told (Genesis 1:27), but clearly each has unique attributes. While some biases and sexist customs sometimes get mixed in, overall country boys are taught to cherish, appreciate, honor, and revere the ladies in their lives. Whether it's their mamas and grannies, their aunts and girl cousins, their classmates and girlfriends, or their dates, wives, and daughters, country boys know how to treat women.

Jesus certainly reflected this in every meeting he had with women. There's another encounter, not at a public watering hole but at someone's house, in which a woman caused a stir. In fact, there are at least three different accounts of this incident in the Gospels, Matthew (chapter 26), Luke (chapter 7), and John (chapter 12). Two of these indicate that it was Mary, Martha and Lazarus's sister, who showed up with an unexpected gift for Jesus. The version that intrigues me the most, however, shows me once more how Jesus treated a woman whom others judged and rejected.

When one of the Pharisees invited Jesus to have dinner with him, he went to the Pharisee's house and reclined at the table. A woman in that town who lived a sinful life learned that Jesus was eating at the Pharisee's house, so she came there with an alabaster jar of perfume. As she stood behind him at his feet weeping, she began to wet his feet with her tears. Then she wiped them with her hair, kissed them and poured perfume on them.

When the Pharisee who had invited him saw this, he said to himself, "If this man were a prophet, he would know who is touching him and what kind of woman she is—that she is a sinner."

Jesus answered him, "Simon, I have something to tell you."

"Tell me, teacher," he said.

"Two people owed money to a certain moneylender. One owed him five hundred denarii, and the other fifty. Neither of them had the money to pay him back, so he forgave the debts of both. Now which of them will love him more?"

Simon replied, "I suppose the one who had the bigger debt forgiven."

"You have judged correctly," Jesus said.

Then he turned toward the woman and said to Simon, "Do you see this woman? I came into your house. You did not give me any water for my feet, but she wet my feet with her tears and wiped them with her hair. You did not give me a kiss, but this woman, from the time I entered, has not stopped kissing my feet. You did not put oil on my head, but she has poured perfume on my feet. Therefore, I tell you, her many sins have been forgiven—as her great love has shown. But who-ever has been forgiven little loves little."

Then Jesus said to her, "Your sins are forgiven."

The other guests began to say among themselves, "Who is this who even forgives sins?"

Jesus said to the woman, "Your faith has saved you; go in peace." (Luke 7:36–50)

There's something so very intimate and beautiful about this scene. One minute Jesus was conversing with this Pharisee who had invited him to his home for dinner. And before he can say, "Pass the potatoes, please," this woman showed up and began to cry. Not only that, but she used her tears to wash Jesus's feet and then dried them with her hair, which she had released from the combs used to keep it pulled back. Finally, she did something that surprised everyone there, everyone except the Lord. She opened a rare, exquisite bottle of perfume and poured it over Jesus's feet.

This perfume in the alabaster jar was most likely something called nard, an oil infused with the floral herb spikenard. Its worth at the time was equal to the average annual salary of most people. Can you imagine spending an entire year's salary on one bottle of perfume? And then can you see yourself taking this incredibly expensive perfume and just pouring it all over someone's feet? Now, I love to give my wife perfume as well as the next man, but that's quite a sacrifice.

But it's exactly what this woman with the bad reputation felt compelled to do. In fact, her sacrificial offering changed the smell in the entire room, perhaps the entire house. Since the Pharisees were not big fans of Jesus, I'm guessing that it may have been somewhat awkward before she arrived. You know, the guests are trying to be polite and not repeat their usual criticisms to Jesus's face. And in walked this bad girl, whom most scholars think was probably a former prostitute, with the most precious gift she owned.

When he sensed his host giving him a judgmental look, Jesus asked this religious leader, Simon, a question: "Who's more appreciative? A person who's been forgiven a debt of a hundred dollars or someone who's had a million-dollar debt wiped away?" It's a rhetorical question with an obvious, commonsense answer, and yet it makes Jesus's point about this woman's motive for doing what she had just done.

Just to make sure that Simon got the point, Jesus did a little comparison. The wealthy, educated, suave, and sophisticated host had not even offered his guest water to wash his feet. This party crasher, a common "sinner," washed Jesus's feet with her tears. While Simon didn't even greet his guest with a gesture of welcome, this woman kissed his feet. And while the Pharisee provided no oil for anointing his guest, this shady lady (yet another one!) brought out the best perfume she had.

Have you ever been to someone's home and sensed that they really didn't like your being there? Sure, they invited you and knew you were coming, but you can tell that they're scrutinizing every little move you make and every word you say so that they can tear you apart later. They're going through the motions of being a good host, but their heart's not in it. Their house may look like a magazine spread and the food tastes like a chef prepared it, but there's no substitute for a true spirit of hospitality.

I'm guessing you know what it feels like to be genuinely welcomed as well. Maybe it was when you dropped in on people unexpectedly and they insisted you stay for dinner, making you feel welcome from the moment you stepped in their home. You might have to step over the kids' toys and the place may not be spotless, but you feel wanted and invited to be yourself there. The food served may not be fancy or be the best you've ever tasted, but you know it's offered generously. Where I come from, we simply call this southern hospitality. And the more I've traveled, the more I've learned to appreciate this gift, because not everyone tries to make others feel welcome.

Simon the Pharisee invited Jesus to dinner so he could figure out what his deal was. And then when this uninvited woman of questionable reputation showed up, it told him all he thought he needed to know about the kind of person Jesus was. But then the tables were turned on him. Because Jesus knew what he was thinking and made it clear that once someone understands grace, then his natural response is to give thanks, to worship, to share his gratitude. They get it. And the scent of their gracious attitude permeates the air around them, just as the self-righteous judgment of religious snobs causes a real stink.

Caught in the Act

Finally, there's a scene that may be the ultimate proof of Jesus's love and compassionate heart toward women. It involves not just a woman with a bad reputation but one actually caught in the act—the immoral act of adultery, that is. A group of religious leaders pounced on her and were preparing to serve as judge, jury, and executioner until Jesus came on the scene. Then this lynch mob thought that it would be even better if they could use this opportunity to trap Jesus as well. They didn't even care so much about what this woman did or why she did it; they were only using her to pounce on their real prey, this man claiming to be God's Son.

At dawn He appeared again in the temple courts, where all the people gathered around him, and he sat down to teach them. The teachers of the law and the Pharisees brought in a woman caught in adultery. They made her stand before the group and said to Jesus, "Teacher, this woman was caught in the act of adultery. In the Law Moses commanded us to stone such women. Now what do you say?" They were using this question as a trap, in order to have a basis for accusing him.

But Jesus bent down and started to write on the

ground with his finger. When they kept on questioning him, he straightened up and said to them, "Let any one of you who is without sin be the first to throw a stone at her." Again he stooped down and wrote on the ground.

At this, those who heard began to go away one at a time, the older ones first, until only Jesus was left, with the woman still standing there. Jesus straightened up and asked her, "Woman, where are they? Has no one condemned you?"

"No one, sir," she said.

"Then neither do I condemn you," Jesus declared. "Go now and leave your life of sin." (John 8:2–11)

Now it's clear that this woman messed up. And it sounds as if she may have been literally dragged from her lover's bed by her accusers. Can't you just see this poor gal's hair all tangled and uncombed, her face tear streaked, clothed in whatever she could grab on her way out the door? Talk about being embarrassed to death!

I'm guessing she knew she'd done something wrong. She probably knew she shouldn't cheat on her spouse or make love to another woman's husband. She messed up. She blew it. She sinned. She made some wrong choices. She deserved to be judged for her moral failure just as much as we all do—because we all fall short of God's standard of perfection. And, thankfully, she encounters a Judge with compassion, mercy, and forgiveness—the very things those condemning her don't know how to offer her.

Have you seen some of these TV shows like *People's Court* or *Judge Judy*? You know, the ones where the plaintiff has some squabble with a neighbor or coworker, a freelance contractor or bill collector? The defendant comes on, adamant that he or she had nothing to do with causing the problem and therefore owes the accuser absolutely nothing. Then the feisty judge kicks in and sets them both straight. You can tell these judges don't take guff from anyone—they're not going to beat around the bush or listen to anyone's bull story. These are not the kind of judges I want to see for a speeding ticket!

Fortunately, this lady caught in adultery did not have to rely on the authority of the people who had caught her. She had an unexpected advocate who presented the most powerful defense ever seen before or since. And it wasn't by his verbal eloquence or clever strategy that he got her accusers to leave. It was simply by writing something in the dust. We don't know what that message was, but I suspect it was something similar to what he finally said: "Let the person without sin cast the first stone." Basically, none of us is fit to judge someone else, not the way only God can, because we can't see into each other's hearts the way he can.

It's also interesting to see the way Jesus addressed this woman. He asked, "Woman, where are your accusers? Isn't anyone going to bring charges against you?" He didn't call her an adulteress or a tramp or any derogatory term at all, some of which might have been accurate under the circumstances. No, he merely forgave her and blessed her life with the gift of God's grace. She might have even seen herself that way, but Jesus made it undeniably clear that she's a free woman, nothing greater and nothing worse.

How about you—ever made some bad choices or done things you regret? I know I sure have. God made a promise to those of us who screw up, the promise of forgiveness and a clean slate. We can have a fresh start if we're willing to accept his gift of grace. It may seem too good to be true, but it's genuinely true, because it's motivated by something that's totally illogical, irrational, and unfathomable—divine love.

Too often I think we beat ourselves up and condemn ourselves even if we're not standing exposed before others. We know how we've failed, where we've lied and cheated, and all our secret sins. And we know that God knows, but still it's hard to believe that he forgives us so fully. But he does. Surely, our own standard can't be higher than God's, can it? Then we have to let go of the burdens of our past and embrace the gift of his grace that leads to our better future.

A Little Respect

Jesus definitely showed that he knew how to treat women, who were already considered subpar citizens in his day. Whether they had a bad reputation, crashed a dinner party, or were caught in an immoral act, he showed them all the same compassionate grace that motivated his every action on this Earth. He was more than willing to risk his reputation so that he might save theirs.

This is what country boys do—they sacrifice themselves in order to treat women like ladies. So many of the stereotypes we see of Jesus, either from church or in the media, depicts him as this meek, mild, frail, skinny guy looking off into the sunset. But I don't buy it. This isn't the image we get when we look at his life in the Bible.

Now, I don't think he was a hell-raising, hard-drinking, woman-chasing wildcat, either, but I know that Jesus was not afraid to stand up to those who were used to pushing others around. He didn't mind mingling with the common man or striking up a socially taboo conversation with a foreign woman. He didn't care if they were virgins or if they'd been with dozens of men. He simply knew that they all needed the same things you and I need—forgiveness, mercy, and love.

Most country boys pride themselves on showing respect to women and conducting themselves in a respectable manner around them. This includes remaining sober, thoughtful, and kind around them. Country boys never offend women with lewd suggestions or vulgar gestures. They never try to grind up against them on the dance floor. Instead, they treat the women they encounter, from their grandmother to the checkout girl at the store to their middle-aged waitress, with the courtesy of a gentleman.

The other night I was out with some friends of ours, and I noticed that every time my friend's wife or mine left or returned to our table, my buddy and I stood up until she had walked away or was seated again. When my friend's wife teased us about it, we told her that we'd been taught that it was good manners for a man always to stand when a lady stood up or approached. My daddy had taught this to me when I was a boy growing up, and I'm already teaching my son the same set of manners. My wife appreciates it and understands that it respects her presence.

Manners like these are not intended to make women feel weak or incapable of doing things for themselves. Most country gals know that they're probably stronger than their boys if they were to arm wrestle! But things like standing or opening doors just shows our respect and the value we place on them as women.

Jesus knew how to treat a lady. Some of them were probably beautiful women, and some may even have tried to flirt with him. But he managed to conduct himself in a way that never reduced their interaction into something crude, sexual, or flirtatious. We're told he was fully human and yet without sin. He continues to set the standard for us today. Sometimes when I hear rap or hip-hop, or any music with lyrics that demean women, I get upset. Even if it's supposedly a "cultural thing," I still think that how we talk about women reflects how we will treat them.

But it wasn't just women he treated with respect. The more I think about it, the more I believe Jesus gives Garth Brooks a run for his money in the crowd he hung around—talk about "friends in low places"! Fishermen, prostitutes, tax collectors, and lepers, just to name a few. He (Jesus, not Garth) showed us how to see each person as a precious, unique individual child of God, made in his image. We are to treat all people with respect, kindness, and compassion.

When we look at the way Christ treated people, we can't get away from the incredible strength, unmerited kindness, and surprising grace of those encounters. He knew that each human being is a masterpiece, created by his Father in his own image. He knew the secret that takes each of us a lifetime to learn—what it really means to love someone.

Chapter Eight

Drivin' and Cryin'—He Knew How It Felt to Have a Broken Heart

If you don't mind a hand me down heart
I've got just the thing for you
It's been bruised and it's been used
But it still beats like new
It's got a few burned valves, it's a little worn-out
But, baby, it'll love you true
So if you don't mind a hand me down heart
I've got one for you
—from "Hand Me Down Heart"

When I was in high school, I had my fair share of dates, crushes, and a couple of girlfriends. There was nothing greater than that warm, wonderful feeling inside that occurred when the pretty girl in my high school agreed to go out with me. I didn't have to be the quarterback for the football team or the homecoming king—the girl I liked also liked me back! That emotional tide washing over me as a teenager was so powerful and so intense that I never wanted it to end.

I soon learned, however, that with "true love" (which I now think of as infatuation and attraction) comes disappointment and that deep, inward, excruciating pain that's called heartache. It's that feeling that your heart, the very center of your being, has not only been abandoned, but dropped off a cliff to shatter into a million shards, like broken glass. The first time I got dumped in high school, I felt like my world had ended and couldn't imagine how I'd ever keep going without that girl whom I had thought was going to be the love of my life. And I felt like a fool for letting myself care so much, for even believing and hoping that she could actually love someone like me. There's nothing like a breakup to trigger every insecurity you've ever had about yourself.

But I lived through that first broken heart and realized that life kept on happening around me and time kept on passing. Slowly, gradually (which was probably all of four days!), I got over her and swore that I'd never put myself in that position again. I rallied with my buddies, had a few drinks, and tried to harden my heart around that tender scar forming inside my chest.

After a while, by the time I was an adult (or at least thought I was), I realized that true love goes deeper than just those teenage crushes and adolescent infatuations. Real relationships require time and a shared history and shared values. Ultimately, it requires trust and a commitment to each other and to what you share together.

As a relatively young man, I thought I had found this kind of bond with a woman that I asked to be my wife. We enjoyed some good times together and produced two beautiful daughters. But then things changed between us, and words were spoken and choices made that neither of us ever expected. It was as if, one day, what had been the sweetest part of my life just dissolved like sugar in a rainstorm.

That time remains one of the darkest, most painful seasons in my life. I gained new insight into what it meant for my heart to break, for it to feel like something deep inside me had been shattered and the fragments lodged in my chest like shrapnel. I truly didn't know if I would ever love again or even want to try. There were so many painful memories and deep scars, and I didn't know how many years it would take for them to heal.

And then I was attending a big awards event in New York City and saw this woman across the room in the hotel's reception area. She was absolutely stunningly beautiful, and there was just something about her, a smile in her eyes, a warmth, a kindness that drew us to each other. Sure enough, we managed to introduce ourselves and get acquainted, and it was as if we'd known each other our whole lives. She was smart and funny and genuine. That conversation led to many more, and, you guessed it, I ended up feeling as smitten as a schoolboy.

Her name was Jessica, and in the course of our conversations, we shared our dreams with each other. When I asked her what she wanted for her life moving forward, she told me she wanted to be a mom. There was an absolute sincerity and innocence to her answer that I loved. Here was this beautiful woman well on her way to a successful career, telling me that she really longed to have a family. Her response sent goose bumps down my back, not because I was looking for an old-fashioned, stay-at-home mom, but because it reflected the true desire of her heart. She told me that she believed God had called her to be a mom and to make home a special place for her husband and children.

A few days before I met Jess, I had just finished reading a book entitled *A Wife After God's Own Heart* by Elizabeth George. I knew I longed to have a special lady in my life with whom to build a life together, but I hadn't done a very good job on my own so far, which is why I read this book. And to meet a beautiful woman, inside and out, who seemed to be echoing the traits I had just read about, less than a week later? It had to be God!

Our romance was a whirlwind. It was better than any Hallmark movie or chick flick at the Cineplex, and I ended up finding love like I'd never dreamed possible. While we're both far from perfect, the relationship we share is unlike anything either of us has ever experienced. There's a level of trust, passion, intimacy, and connection that is so much bigger than us that it has to come from God. And I suspect it's something that we could never have shared without first experiencing the pain of a broken heart.

When a Man Cries

Now even though Jesus never got involved with a woman in a romantic relationship, even though he never dated or was engaged or married, it doesn't mean that he never experienced a broken heart. In fact, I'm convinced that he knew what it felt like to have his heart broken in a way that goes way beyond what we tend to think of as heartache. For you see, Jesus loved people, perfectly and selflessly, and this kind of divine love has no selfish motives or hidden agendas involved. Which, in my book, means it only hurt all the more when he lost someone.

And perhaps the most dramatic scene where it's clear that Jesus felt a keen sense of grief involved the death of his good friend Lazarus. Most of us learned to recite the shortest verse in the Bible, "Jesus wept" (John 11:35), in Sunday school without realizing all that was packed into those two words. From my experience, it's pretty amazing for a grown man to cry. Most of us were taught not to show our tears and display such raw emotion in front of others. So for a guy to allow the tears to fall—and not just any guy but the Son of God—well, it must have been an intensely painful event.

I mean, really, if you think about it, what in the world could cause Jesus to lose it? There were certainly times in his life when I could understand if he had cried, especially during all the abuse he suffered leading up to the crucifixion. But the reason "Jesus wept" wasn't because of his own physical suffering, but due to the loss of someone he loved dearly.

As the brother of Mary and Martha, Lazarus must have gotten to hang around Jesus quite a bit. Except for the disciples, no one else is mentioned spending as much time with him as these three adult siblings. And in order to evoke tears from the Son of God, you know they had to have been close friends. The really curious thing about this situation, though, is that Jesus cries over a loss he clearly could've prevented.

A Little Too Late

Apparently, Jesus and the disciples were traveling around when the two sisters sent him an urgent message, "Lord, the one you love is sick" (John 11:3). That's the kind of news that none of us likes to receive, like a phone call in the middle of the night. You just know that it's not going to be good, and you only hope that you get to your loved one in time. And if anyone could've gotten there with time to spare, you'd think Jesus surely could have.

But Jesus stayed put where he was for two more days and continued teaching, preaching, and healing the many people who had come to see him. When he's finally ready to return to Judea to see his sick friend, the disciples raised the possibility of another problem. "But Rabbi," they said, "a short while ago the Jews there tried to stone you, and yet you are going back?" (John 11:8). Undaunted by this possibility, Jesus replied, "Our friend Lazarus has fallen asleep; but I am going there to wake him up" (John 11:11).

Now his followers were really confused and wondered if he meant that their friend was literally asleep. So Jesus then makes the situation crystal clear: "Lazarus is dead, and for your sake I am glad I was not there, so that you may believe. But let us go to him" (John 11:14–15). Without a doubt, he knew what was going on and indicates that he has waited for a bigger purpose—"so that you may believe." Which is amazing to me, since I'm guessing that the human part of Jesus wanted to rush to his friend and do something.

It's like when my kids are sick and the doctor tells us there's nothing to do but wait it out. As their daddy who loves them more than anything, I want to do something—anything—to make them feel better. But the only way for them to get well in some cases is to do nothing, which feels excruciating. This seems significant to me because it reveals just how much Christ was willing to suffer for the sake of those he loved. Not just one person, but everyone he loved.

When they finally arrived at his friends' home in Bethany, Lazarus had been dead for *four* days. Wow—can't you just imagine what his family must've been thinking and feeling? Here they have a friend who's the Son of God and can do anything, and they've sent word almost a week ago about the dire situation they're in. And then they heard nothing in response. So their brother dies and is buried. Somehow their pain had to have felt more acute knowing that Someone literally could've done something if he had chosen to.

See How He Loved

It's one thing to lose a loved one, but to lose him knowing that a friend could've healed him if only he'd arrived in time? That had to be salt in the wound of their grief. Mary and Martha had to have wondered if Jesus was really their friend and cared anything about them. Why else would he have lingered on the road when he knew they needed him?

And it's clear the two sisters are indeed upset with Jesus for not getting there sooner. Martha saw him approaching and rushed out to meet Christ and the disciples. She said, "If you had been here, my brother would not have died. But I know that even now God will give you whatever you ask" (John 11:21–22). It seems to me that she might've been trying to lay a little guilt trip on Jesus, both indicating her disappointment as well as a ray of hope that he still could do something.

Her sister, Mary, on the other hand, stayed at home until finally Jesus asked for her. When this woman and others came out to meet him, they were crying and obviously still soaked in grief. We're told that when he saw the many mourners, Jesus was "deeply moved in spirit and troubled" (John 11:33).

Jesus then asked Mary where Lazarus had been buried, and she told him to follow her. This was when Jesus couldn't hold back any longer and the floodgate of his tears finally opened. Before they had even arrived at his friend's tomb, the Lord's tears began to fall. And each drop spoke volumes about how much he cared, how much he suffered, how much he regretted the pain that his late arrival caused. The Jewish mourners said, "See how he loved him!" (John 11:36), even though they probably wondered how the Messiah who could heal lepers and give sight to the blind didn't arrive in time to prevent his friend from dying.

Jesus certainly could have—and maybe he even wanted to heal Lazarus while he was sick in order to spare them all the intense heartache that occurred instead. However, there was a bigger story unfolding. He knew that his Father would be glorified and more people would hear about the miracle if he arrived after his friend had died and been buried.

And no matter how much Martha and the others might've hoped that Jesus would do something unbelievably dramatic, I'm guessing no one was prepared for what happened next. There at Lazarus's tomb, Christ commanded his friend to come out. For the dead man, I wonder if it was like waking up and not being able to get out from under the covers, for we're told: "The dead man came out, his hands and feet wrapped with strips of linen, and a cloth around his face" (John 11:44). Jesus had the mourners remove the burial clothes from Lazarus and set him free. Death no longer had a hold on him. The man's lifeless, cold body suddenly came to life. His heart started beating, his lungs started pumping, and blood began to course through his body.

Always on Time

I'm convinced that Jesus waited until after his friend had died for two reasons besides the one he mentioned. In addition to its glorifying God, this scene also displays just how incredibly human Jesus was. Here he was, only seconds away from resurrecting Lazarus, and yet he can't hold back the wave of sorrow washing over him. He felt the depth of their loss, their pain, their heartache. Jesus allowed his heart to break into pieces just like everyone else's did who was there and loved Lazarus.

God is not an unfeeling God, trying to force us into complying with his strict guidelines so that he can spoil our fun.

He is a God who sees our pain and suffering and knows what it's like to lose the love of those who mean the world to him. Our Father keeps his promises and knows what it's like to experience the raw depths of loss that we go through. We may not understand why certain things happen in our lives, why certain prayers are answered the way we want and why others aren't. But we should never for a second stop believing that he cares about us.

The other point we must notice from this scene is that God's power continues to bring new life to us today. We may be challenged with a physical disease such as MS or battling an addiction that threatens to destroy our lives. Whether it's our marriage, our kids, or our desire to find a new job, the Lord continues to call us out of our tombs of despair and bring us back to life. Jesus came to call us forth to a life of genuine purpose and meaningful relationships. He doesn't want us entangled in the grave clothes of our past mistakes.

Our dreams may have died and we may feel as if our hearts have lost their ability to feel alive. But Jesus never gives up on us. I think of an old saying of my grandmother's: "God may not come when you want him to, but he's always on time." Broken hearts don't stay broken forever; God collects the pieces and makes a mosaic more beautiful than the original.

Making the Cut

The death of Lazarus may be the only time that the Bible tells us that Jesus wept, but I suspect there were other moments when his sense of loss was just as great. One in particular seems to have left him with that wistful, sad feeling of wondering what might have been. You see, someone came to see him to ask a very important question, which he gladly answered. Unfortunately, though, Jesus's response was not what his visitor wanted to hear.

A certain ruler asked him, "Good teacher, what must I do to inherit eternal life?"

"Why do you call me good?" Jesus answered. "No one is good—except God alone. You know the commandments: 'You shall not commit adultery, you shall not murder, you shall not steal, you shall not give false testimony, honor your father and mother.'"

"All these I have kept since I was a boy," he said.

When Jesus heard this, he said to him, "You still lack one thing. Sell everything you have and give to the poor, and you will have treasure in heaven. Then come, follow me."

*When he heard this, he became very sad, because he
was very wealthy. Jesus looked at him and said, "How
hard it is for the rich to enter the kingdom of God!
Indeed, it is easier for a camel to go through the eye of a
needle than for someone who is rich to enter the kingdom of God." (Luke 18:18–25)*

While it's clear that the rich man was sad when Jesus
asked him to give away all his wealth, I suspect that Jesus
was also sad, based on the figurative language he uses to
make his point. Their exchange had started as a discussion
of what it means to be "good enough" to know God. Jesus
made it clear that no one is good enough, ironically asking
the ruler, "Why do you call me good?" It's almost as if he's
challenging the man to define what it means to consider
oneself good.

Interestingly enough, if it had been just a matter of keeping the commandments and following the Jewish religious
laws, then the man would've made the cut. He said that he
had kept all these rules since he was a boy. In response, Jesus
told him that there's only one thing left then, to sell all he
has and follow him.

Apparently, though, the rich man just couldn't agree to
this final requirement. And I don't think it's a matter of

Jesus's wanting the guy's money (like a bad televangelist) or even wanting him to give to those less fortunate. I believe Jesus knew that there was only one idol left that could possibly prevent this man from enjoying a close relationship with God, and therefore, being considered "good." The point that Jesus made is that if one relies on his money for his security, then he might miss out on recognizing his spiritual poverty. No matter how much money a person has, it can never buy his or her way into a relationship with God or into heaven.

Jesus isn't saying that it's impossible for the rich to get into heaven—remember, nothing's impossible with God—but only that their wealth prevents them from seeing how needy they are. Believe me, I get this point loud and clear. Even in the midst of my success, I always give God thanks and know that he is the only One who provides it. Now, I certainly do my best to work hard and give all that I've got to maximize the gifts that he's given me. But the many blessings I have in life are only because of his goodness.

And while I'm grateful for the many material blessings I have, I'm reminded daily that people are what matter most to God. This is one of the important life lessons I try to teach my kids each day as well. My son, who is like me in so many different ways, likes to keep his toys neat and his room clean (we'll see how long that lasts!). He takes pride in his things and sometimes has a hard time sharing with his sister or other kids. So his mother and I remind him that "things" don't matter nearly as much as people do. Things get lost or broken, we outgrow them, or they lose their appeal or usefulness. If we're putting our hope in possessions, then enough is never enough. Jesus asked, "What good is it for a man to gain the world yet forfeit his soul?" (Mark 8:36). We can certainly enjoy the blessing in our lives, but ultimately God wants us to invest in relationships with others.

That's why I try to give back as much as I can for all kinds of causes, from finding a cure for MS to feeding the homeless. I know what it's like to go without what everyone else takes for granted, and my humble beginnings will always be with me. Growing up in the country keeps me humble and grateful for everything I've ever received.

Breaking God's Heart

I'm convinced that it's not just relying on money for our security that breaks God's heart. He's devastated anytime we choose something else to try to fill the place inside us that only he can satisfy. When we rely on money or technology or our career achievements or another person or fame—or whatever it may be—instead of realizing that only he can meet our needs, then we basically become idolaters.

You see, Jesus wasn't the only One who knew what it was like to be heartbroken over the people he loved. His Father had been doing it since Adam and Eve blew it back in the Garden of Eden! They used their gift of free will to do the only thing God had asked them not to do. They took a bite out of the forbidden fruit and bought a ticket into a world that's continued to suffer the consequences of their selfish choice ever since.

As if this rough beginning wasn't hard enough, God tried to connect with his people, but they just wouldn't listen to him or honor him. Eventually, God had his heart broken when people apparently forgot all about him—well, everyone except Noah—and so he decided to flood the Earth and start over.

God even had his heart broken after he rescued the Children of Israel out of slavery in Egypt. While Moses was up on a mountaintop, jotting down the Ten Commandments on stone tablets, the Israelites were taking their jewelry and melting it down to make a golden calf, an idol that they began to worship. Think about that for a moment! God has done all kinds of miraculous things to get them out of bondage—from bringing on plagues to parting the Red Sea—and this is how they end up thanking him.

Unfortunately, it didn't get any better once they arrived in the Promised Land, after God had helped them defeat their enemies and take possession of their new home. Despite all God had done for them, they continued to do their own thing, worshipping pagan gods, and disobeying the Lord's instructions. They just didn't get it, or they didn't want to get it. They seemed very content in breaking their Creator's heart—so much so that God, who had been speaking through people he selected to be his prophets, chose a spokesman to experience the same kind of situation himself.

"When the Lord began to speak through Hosea, the Lord said to him, 'Go marry a promiscuous woman and have children with her, for like an adulterous wife this land is guilty of unfaithfulness to the Lord'" (Hosea 1:2). Yep, you read that right! As crazy unbelievable as it sounds, God told his main man Hosea to go marry a woman not exactly known for her high standards and constant fidelity.

I mean, if I were Hosea, I'm going to be saying, "Uh, excuse me, Lord? What did you just say? Go and marry whom?" These prophets were usually holy men, often priests at the temple, who had dedicated their lives to serving God. To marry at all would have been a bit surprising, but to marry a woman known to make her living by selling her body to men for sex, well, that was unimaginable. Old

Hosea must have been shaking his head and wondering if he had eaten some bad fish tacos the night before!

But he had heard correctly, and the second part of the message was perhaps even more devastating than the first. Not only was Hosea to marry a prostitute, but he was to be prepared for her to conceive children that were not his. Can you imagine? And maybe the craziest thing of all is that Hosea's name, like all Hebrew names, carried great significance. It's meaning? *Salvation.*

Turn Up the Volume

The first time I read the book of Hosea, I was stunned and couldn't believe how crazy it sounded. But the more I reread it and did a little studying and talking to people who know about the Bible, the more I realized that it was intended to get our attention, just as it was intended to get the Israelites' attention then. God had done everything in his power to make the relationship work with his children. He had tried talking to them, had delivered them from Egyptian slavery, had provided food and water for them while hiking through the desert for forty years, had made his rules for them to follow prominent and clear. And yet still they turned their backs on him.

In this new land they had overtaken, Canaan, there were a lot of other tribes who worshipped stone idols and false gods. They were superstitious. Instead of the Israelites teaching them about the True God, they turned away from him and joined in the pagan worship of their new land. It almost seemed like no matter what God did to get their attention, they still ignored him. Nothing was enough.

However, as noted writer and theologian C. S. Lewis once commented, pain is "God's megaphone to rouse a deaf world." Apparently, we often don't hear him—or want to hear him—when things are going well or when he merely whispers. In desperate times, people usually realize that they have nowhere else to turn but to the Almighty. Pain turns up the volume on our ability to listen for God. But it can take a while to get to that place.

And in the meantime, God wanted to get everyone's attention. They had already ignored what some of his other prophets had said. So now it was time to speak not only through words but through actions. He would have his prophet, his representative to his nation, act out what God himself was experiencing. Basically, what it was like to be in love with someone who stubbornly refused to be faithful.

It's almost as if God said, "This will illustrate how Israel has acted like a prostitute by turning against the Lord and worshiping other gods" (my paraphrase of Hosea 1:2).

As strange as it may sound to us, God loved his people so much that he wanted them to realize how painful it was for them to crush his heart. He wanted them to realize that while he was God, he was not above feeling the deep, immense anguish of a broken heart. In many ways, this kind of drastic action serves as the precursor of the ultimate sacrifice God would make on behalf of all people. To send his one and only Son, Jesus, into our world as a human. To allow his Son, whom he loves more than we can imagine, to be nailed to some beams of wood and die one of the most painful, agonizing deaths possible.

Repeatedly throughout both the Old and New Testaments, God is obsessed with loving us. He's not going to let us go. He's always going to come after us, welcome us home, clean us up and hold us tight. Even when we betray him again. And this is the scene at the home of the prophet Hosea and his wife, Gomer.

As I mentioned, for their marriage to take place in the first place was nothing short of a miracle. Here's a man at the top of their culture, a man of God, choosing a woman at the bottom of society. Based on the cultural practices of the day, it was a kind of business transaction, so Gomer's father was probably thrilled to have someone take her off his hands, especially since she was used goods.

The other interesting thing about the story of Hosea and Gomer, so I discovered, is that this is the first time that God compares his relationship to us as a marriage in the Bible. And here he makes it loud and clear that it's not just a figure of speech but something every bit as real as the love between a bride and groom—and the heartbreak when she betrays her man.

After the story of Hosea and Gomer, the marriage metaphor gets used many times, by Jesus and John and Paul. In the New Testament, the church is often described as the Bride of Christ, preparing for the big day when he will return for the ultimate celebration of their special relationship. "Let us rejoice and be glad . . . ! For the wedding of the Lamb has come, and his bride has made herself ready" (Revelation 19:7).

The Price of Grace

What I love about the painful story of Hosea and Gomer is that God makes it clear how much we mean to him. It's not just about our following his rules and regulations and

JESUS WAS A COUNTRY BOY

trying to earn his approval—as if we could if we tried. No, it's about a real heart-and-soul kind of intimate relationship, one that's genuine and honest, open and vulnerable. In my way of thinking, the story of Hosea and Gomer reminds us that knowing God has nothing to do with religion and everything to do with an authentic relationship.

Now it's easy to criticize organized religion, especially in our country, for being too political, too critical, or too judgmental. Maybe you're like me and cringe sometimes when you're flipping channels and see fire-and-brimstone televangelists begging for money and promising miracles in exchange for donations. Maybe you've been disappointed by attending church or even burned by someone's hypocritical actions. While it's tempting to give up on God when such moments occur, it's important to remember that these things do not accurately reflect who he is.

Religion is man-made, an attempt to put God in a box and have everything figured out so that you can feel good about yourself and better than other people. At its worst, religion tries to make our interactions with God like a cosmic kind of business transaction. If we do the "right things," such as give our time, money, and attention to his causes (or what other so-called believers claim are his causes), then we can expect a good job, plenty of money, a loving spouse, and healthy kids.

But this isn't the way it works, and the people who keep trying to convince you it is really make me mad. They have an agenda that's not God's agenda. Grace isn't grace until it's poured into empty hands. When you empty yourself of yourself, then you can be filled with God's grace. No one deserves it; that's the point. Why should anyone boast? No one can!

The only agenda God has is to love his children and to help them understand who he is and who they are. Jesus didn't come to this Earth to start a new religious craze called Christianity. He came to restore our ability to connect with his Father by dying for our sins. He came to do something that we could never do no matter how hard we tried. He sacrificed himself so that we could have it all. "Greater love has no one than this: to lay down one's life for one's friends" (John 15:13). Pain reminds us that while grace is free, it's never cheap.

CHAPTER NINE

Grace Amazing—He Gave It All for the Sake of Love

From the southern tip of Texas
To the top of Bangor, Maine
Those Friday night lights at those hometown games
Man, they mean everything
—FROM "ALL AMERICAN"

As I'm writing this book, it's an election year, and the many candidates are constantly in the news, often for swinging verbal punches at each other. While the campaign speeches continue and the news media dissects every word, twitch, and punctuation mark, I'm guessing I'm not the only one who gets weary of the process. There seems to be a lot of accusations and mudslinging and not as much honor and integrity on display.

Now, don't get me wrong—I love our country as much as any other red-blooded American. I'm proud of our nation and grateful that we have a democratic system of government where we get to vote for whoever we believe to be most qualified to represent us. It's just that, well, sometimes it seems like the politicians are fighting for their own agendas or their party's agendas more than the needs of the people they represent.

However, there's a large group of individuals who I know without a doubt are fighting for their love of country and dedication to its foundation of democracy. They are the men and women of our U.S. military teams, serving both at home and around the world. From the very founding of our country over two hundred years ago, the American people have been taking risks, upholding their beliefs, and sacrificing everything they have—even their very lives—to defend the freedom that we all hold so dear.

This courage and tenacity has been tested time and time again throughout the many wars, battles, and military engagements in which we've had to fight. We even faced the most heart-wrenching experience of all in which brother fought against brother in the War Between the States, the U.S. Civil War. Then in the twentieth century, our nation found itself on the front lines of international conflict, participating and ultimately leading a victorious charge in both world wars. The Korean War, Vietnam, and most recently battles in the Middle East have cost us so many lives, all given to protect our country and our way of life.

After the unimaginable, horrifying assault of 9/11, we faced a new kind of enemy. Unlike the ones our fathers and grandfathers faced in earlier battles defending our country, these terrorists tried to cut us off at the knees here on our own soil. And while the terrible toll of human lives will never be forgotten, it was our unity that ultimately defined us. In the end, it was the ongoing dedication to defend our nation by thousands and thousands of men and women in uniform that has kept us standing strong as "the home of the brave and the land of the free."

These courageous soldiers risk their lives on a daily basis to protect the homes that they have been forced to leave behind temporarily. Their equally courageous wives, husbands, children, and families also make sacrifices that demand immense respect, abiding gratitude, and our ongoing support. It's a sacrifice that I'm afraid too many of us take for granted.

I'm always excited to play in a concert where I know a majority of people attending are from our armed forces. It's a small thing, but I try to give them an extra dose of enthusiasm along with an extra song or two. I'm so grateful for our veterans and the ways they have given their lives to protecting our country and its values. I hear a lot these days about how our world is starving for heroes, but all we have to do to find some real ones is look around.

From my experience, many of these men and women know what it means to be country, whether they're from the city, the suburbs, or somewhere in between. Like you and me, they know that country is a state of mind and that living a life of honesty, integrity, and liberty unites us all in our nation's family of freedom. Many of them also know how important it is to have faith while in the foxholes and firefights.

Like a Good Neighbor

These soldiers know that the ultimate role model for all of us is Jesus, the One who made the most amazing sacrifice of all time, one who continues to give life and express his love even today. Because he knew the depths of his Father's love, Jesus could lay down his life for us all so that we can know the extent of God's love as well. He taught us the key to living like a good old country boy: loving our neighbors, forgiving our enemies, and giving all we've got to gain what we can never lose.

While the stereotype of the Hatfields and the McCoys and other "feuding hillbillies" might come to mind when you think about your neighbors in the country, most people know that in order to survive, we have to rely on one another. Sure, country people are independent and often very self-sufficient, but they also know when it's time to lend a helping hand or to ask for one themselves.

As I shared earlier about my upbringing, we were out in the middle of nowhere, miles from the nearest town and even farther from the big city of Houston. Even our closest neighbor was about a half mile across the pasture and through the wood, so we had to rely on ourselves and worked hard to get everything done that needed doing. But we still knew that we could count on our neighbors when we needed help. When a fence breaks down and the bull gets loose, a good neighbor helps you get the bull back in the barn and fix the fence.

In the summertime, when the harvest comes in and you're running out your ears with tomatoes, cucumbers, and squash, no self-respecting country boy or gal is going to let those go to waste. Instead, they take a big mess of them in a paper bag or wicker basket over to the neighbor's house. And often in return they come home with a bag of apples or sack of new potatoes. If a truck breaks down or a tractor needs a part, then neighbors provide a ride into town to the mechanic's or the feed store.

Little country churches often know better than anyone what it means to be a good neighbor. They make sure that the kids in their community have school supplies come August or winter coats before the first frost comes. They collect canned goods and food staples for the church pantry that provides groceries for people in the area who are out of work or down on their luck. Many of these little country churches provide mother's-day-out programs and meals for senior citizens.

Jesus made it clear that this is what loving God is all about—loving and serving each other. When some of the religious leaders tried to trap him by asking which commandments and religious laws were most important, Christ told them that really it only boiled down to a couple. Which shocked the Pharisees and self-righteous religious folks listening because they had memorized hundreds and hundreds of such laws, most of them not even from the Bible but of their own making.

But Jesus said, "'Love the Lord your God with all your heart and with all your soul and with all your mind.' This is the first and greatest commandment. And the second is like it: 'Love your neighbor as yourself.' All the Law and the Prophets hang on these two commandments" (Matthew 22:37–40).

A Little Extra

Now, I realize that loving our neighbors as ourselves doesn't come easy. Even when my kids were very young, I remember watching them at times on the playground, stubbornly refusing to share their toys. Which made me kind of sad the first time I witnessed it, but then I realized that really I'm no different. None of us is. All of us want what we want the way we want it, and when we want it!

Which means that loving our neighbors requires some effort on our part. First, it means being willing to accept and respect people—even when they're different from us or when we don't particularly like them. I remember hearing an elderly man once pray, "Lord, help those who are young and prone to making foolish choices. Help those who are working hard and don't know how to keep going. And help those who are old and tired and need some rest. At some point in our lives, we'll all be in one of those places, so, Lord, help us to have compassion on everyone we meet today."

Needless to say, his prayer stuck with me. I've remembered it when a young kid cuts me off on the highway and then has the crazy nerve to flip me off! Or when a buddy of mine seems to be having a midlife crisis and backs out of a business deal he and I have made. Or when an old lady a few rows ahead of me takes her time getting to her feet and getting off a plane. You never know what a small act of kindness can do to change a person's entire day. And you never know when you're going to need to have a bad day changed in your own life.

Think for a moment about how something as small as a warm, genuine smile can make you feel welcome, even if it's from a stranger—the waitress in the restaurant or the cashier in the convenience store. A phone call or even a quick text from a friend for no other reason than he or she was thinking of you can remind you that you're not alone. An unexpected gift, no matter how small, tells its receiver that you were thinking of him, that you noticed him, that you care about him.

My wife, who's from New Orleans, told me there's a great Cajun word for this kind of attitude, *lagniappe*, which means "just a little extra." It's getting an extra doughnut when you buy a dozen or receiving a free sweatshirt when you join the gym (and you may need to, after all those extra doughnuts!). It's bringing your hostess a bottle of her favorite wine and showing that you remembered what she loves.

Lagniappe is an attitude of going the extra mile and doing it with no hidden agenda—just gratitude and appreciation. It's the approach I try always to take with my fans when they stop me in public and ask for an autograph or want to shoot the breeze. I want them to know how much I appreciate them and their support of my music. I want them to know that I don't take them for granted and think that I'm some sort of stuck-up star.

When we practice being good neighbors, others are able to see God's love shining through us. When we choose to remember that we're not the center of the world and that other people need our help, then it keeps us humble, honest, and happier than we would be otherwise. The example Jesus set for us makes it clear that noticing other people is what it's all about—caring about them, serving their needs, and consistently forgiving them.

Forgive and Forget

Perhaps there's no greater way to show how much we love others than by our willingness to forgive them. In fact, we may never have our love tested until we're put in a situation where we have to choose to forgive someone—and it's definitely a choice, no matter how painful it may feel. Not that we just say a quick "I forgive you" and then pretend to forget, acting like nothing ever happened. No, Jesus made it clear that in order to forgive someone, we have to be aware of what we ourselves have been forgiven.

One of his disciples once asked him, "'Lord, how many times shall I forgive my brother or sister who sins against me? Up to seven times?' Jesus answered, 'I tell you, not seven times, but seventy-seven times'" (Matthew 18:21–22). He then followed up his answer with the parable of the wicked slave, a guy who begs forgiveness on his huge debt from his wealthy master, which he was granted. But then he turns around and demands payment in full on a nickel-and-dime loan from a guy with less than he has. When the slave's master found out, he was furious and had the loser thrown in jail. The grace and mercy that the master had given him meant nothing apparently since he refused to show it to someone else for a much smaller debt.

Jesus made the message to all of us loud and clear then: "This is how my heavenly Father will treat each of you unless you forgive your brother or sister from your heart" (Matthew 18:35). Making mistakes, choosing selfishly, and putting our agendas first are all part of what it means to be human. Which means we all have to learn to ask for forgiveness in our lives as well as receive it. And these two dimensions of forgiveness are two sides of the same coin: our ability to ask for forgiveness is tied to our ability to forgive others. Jesus made this just as clear in the Lord's Prayer as he did in this parable.

He said we are to ask our Father to "forgive us our debts

as we also have forgiven our debtors" (Matthew 6:12). Just as the wicked slave should've realized how much he'd been forgiven, we, too, need to recognize the immense debt that we owe to God for giving us his Son. It's clear that we've all sinned and missed the mark of what it requires to be as holy and perfect as our Father (Romans 3:23). And for thousands of years, the way to deal with this was to make animal sacrifices as a symbol of the human need for God's cleansing.

But then God sent his Son as the ultimate sacrifice. When Christ died on the cross, he did away with the human need ever to sacrifice animals again. We now had access to God's divine, cleaning mercy once and for all. We only have to receive it. And when we embrace God's grace, then we're going to want to forgive others the same way. We're going to want them to taste some of what we've tasted, the relief, the freedom, the joy at being unburdened by the weight of our past mistakes.

God can and will forgive us and make us clean. In fact, he does it over and over and over again. His mercy, grace, and love toward us are so great that he never gives up on us, no matter how many times we continue to mess up. God knows the bad habits, the secret addictions, the hidden things going on in our life right now, those areas that we're not proud of, those places filled with guilt and shame. But we don't have to get stuck in the quicksand of all those mistakes.

Paid in Full

No matter what we've done, or even what we're still doing, God can forgive us! Even the worst things that we can think of—even murder or rape or adultery or betrayal—are not bigger than God's grace. Nothing we ever do is too big. He gives us hundreds of second chances and cleanses us of every sin, every failure, every offense that we've ever committed. He doesn't want us to use his mercy and kindness as an excuse to keep doing things our own way, but to realize the enormous love he has for us.

Unlike some of us, God doesn't forgive partially. He doesn't hold grudges or remember in the back of his mind those things we said. When he forgives us, it's wiped away. He doesn't remember our sins anymore. "As far as the east is from the west, so far has he removed our transgressions from us" (Psalm 103:12). It doesn't take a country boy to know that no matter how hard you try, east and west can never meet. Once God has forgiven you, all your sins are completely removed.

I've heard preachers, counselors, and doctors—not to mention a few country singers—explain that we're only hurting ourselves when we refuse to forgive. Bitterness and resentment form when we refuse to forgive, and those things are poison, my friend. They will eat your heart and soul up and consume everything in your life if you let them. When we end up feeling offended or mistreated, we easily slide into a victim's mentality, feeling sorry for ourselves and wanting to take vengeance into our own hands.

But this isn't God's way of doing things. And that's why he brings it back to what's going on inside our own hearts and lives. We may not have murdered someone, but we've hated them and gossiped about their reputations. We may not have committed adultery, but we've lusted after someone else's spouse and fantasized about being with her behind closed doors. We may not have embezzled funds from our employer, but we've taken home a box of office supplies. None of us is perfect, and if there's breath in us, then we all have the capacity to be selfish, manipulative, and deceitful.

That's why Jesus tells us in the Lord's Prayer that we ask for these things, including (or maybe especially) forgiveness, on a daily basis. While our salvation is secured once and for all, to keep the relationship healthy, we need to confess to God what we've done and ask his forgiveness. It's not that he doesn't already know what we've done, but it's for our benefit. Sometimes, it's really hard to forgive ourselves and to believe that we've done what we did or said what we said.

If you don't feel forgiven, then it's going to be tough to give others what you haven't experienced in your own life. It would be like my trying to write a love song without ever having loved anyone in my own life. It seems to me that so many people, including a lot of Christians, walk around with this cloud over their heads. They're burdened by secrets, bound by shame, and shackled by guilt. They continue to condemn themselves and hold themselves to a standard of judgment that is not God's. Too many people don't seem to realize that God has set them free and forgiven them. No wonder it's so hard for them to show compassion and forgive and release other people when they can't accept it for themselves. Jesus reminds us, "Freely you have received; freely give" (Matthew 10:8).

How do we move forward then? Even when we're battling our own emotions or we don't feel forgiven, we must remember that forgiveness is a choice. Our feelings may come and go like the weather, but God's truth is real and timeless. We simply have to keep choosing to accept his amazing grace. We can't save ourselves; we need God's pardon, which he so freely gives when we ask him.

Thank goodness that his forgiveness is not conditional on anything we do! It's free even though it's not cheap. Jesus paid the price completely, not just in part. He didn't go through all the pain and suffering of dying on the cross so that he could pay the price of our sins with an installment plan! No, Jesus paid it all, taking your sin and my sin on that cross. He paid in full and canceled our debt.

Mercy is like a mighty river. If we swim with the current of God's forgiveness, then we can flow on the tide of forgiveness, bringing its healing waters to everyone we encounter. If we stop forgiving, the river dries up and we get stuck in the mud. We have to be willing to release so that we can receive. If our fists are clenched and our hands are squeezing someone else's neck, then we can't very well receive what God gives us. We have to let the past go if we want to receive what the future holds. "Be kind and compassionate to one another, forgiving each other, just as in Christ God forgave you" (Ephesians 4:32).

At Your Service

I've been privileged to tour and perform around the world, and I'm always impressed to see how God is working in other cultures and countries. In some cases, the government, popular culture, and even their families may be against them, but people wanting to know God are risking it all to read their Bibles, study his Word together, and worship with other like-minded believers. In some countries—such as China—every time they meet they're risking arrest and possible jail time. Many people risk their lives to smuggle in Bibles and to train others in its teachings.

Even in the Western world—such as the United Kingdom and European countries—where Christians are not overtly persecuted, many of the believers there are clearly serious about their faith. Living in a post-Christian culture where faith traditions such as praying or attending church are considered to be old-fashioned, for the uneducated, and even to be superstitious, these people make enormous sacrifices to know God and worship him openly. Without social acceptance or any kind of cultural encouragement, they know that following the example of Jesus will be challenging at best.

In our own country, some Christian leaders and many pastors fear that we might be headed in a similar declining direction with looser morals, fewer standards, and greater power for media in popular culture. I can understand their concern, but maybe this wouldn't be such a bad thing. Sometimes we have to lose something before we no longer take it for granted. We may be straddling the fence on an issue or a cause until something happens to push us to one side or the other. I'm convinced most of us, being the good country boys and gals we are, are up for a fight when it's the right fight.

When our children and their futures are affected, we're willing to stand up. When someone tries to step on our national toes and encroach on our freedom, then we're not backing down from a fight. When one group or denomination or person tries to tell us that they've cornered the market on God's Truth, then we're not afraid to speak our minds and make our own beliefs clear. And when people are in need in our own backyard, we're not going to hesitate to lend a helping hand and do all that we can to help them back on their feet.

I believe that this is what sacrificial giving and joyful living is all about. Christians are called to show other people the love of God and not just talk about it. Some people get hung up on how a certain Bible verse is translated and interpreted. And others are known by what they're against more than what they're for. Isn't it time once again that as Christians we become known by our love? Following Jesus and living a life of faith takes practice. Like being country, it's a way of life, an attitude, an ongoing series of lifestyle habits based on practicing what you preach.

It sure seems to me that loving God and obeying what he says in the Bible is nothing if not practical. Over and over again, it's clear that God cares about the details of our lives. "Look at the birds of the air; they do not sow or reap or store away in barns, and yet your heavenly Father feeds them. Are you not much more valuable than they? Can any one of you by worrying add a single hour to your life?" (Matthew 6:26–27).

It's no big surprise that if we look at the life of Jesus, we see that he ministered to those around him in very practical, physical ways. He turned water into wine at a wedding reception in Cana. He blessed a couple of fish and some loaves of bread and turned it into Filet-O-Fish for five thousand people. He healed lepers with his touch. He spit in the mud and healed the blind with it. He washed the feet of his disciples. He served them bread and wine at their last meal together before his death. And he returned to cook them breakfast on the beach.

Service with a Smile

Jesus repeatedly told his followers—and it still applies for us today—that we should put our faith into practice by serving the physical needs of others and not just the spiritual. In fact, the two—physical and spiritual—seem to go hand in hand. When asked who would be with him in heaven, Jesus explained by describing what those people will have been known for—not their words but their actions.

" 'For I was hungry and you gave me something to eat, I
was thirsty and you gave me something to drink, I was a
stranger and you invited me in, I needed clothes and you
clothed me, I was sick and you looked after me, I was in
prison and you came to visit me.'

"Then the righteous will answer him, 'Lord, when did
we see you hungry and feed you, or thirsty and give you
something to drink? When did we see you a stranger and
invite you in, or needing clothes and clothe you? When
did we see you sick or in prison and go to visit you?'

"The King will reply, 'I tell you the truth, whatever
you did for one of the least of these brothers of mine, you
did for me.'" (Matthew 25:35–40)

Despite what the religious leaders in Jesus's day had done
to create a legalistic, exclusive kind of club, God had always
made it clear that he was the God of all and that he took
care of all his children, not just a few. From the time the
Israelites wandered in the desert following their bondage in
Egypt until the time of Jesus's birth, the Bible consistently
revealed how people should act—with kindness, generosity,
and compassion for all people. In the Old Testament, we see
references like these, indicating that God indeed cares about
how everyone is treated:

- "Do not take advantage of the widow or the father-less" (Exodus 22:22).
- "He defends the cause of the fatherless and the widow, and loves the foreigner residing among you, giving them food and clothing" (Deuteronomy 10:18).
- "A father to the fatherless, a defender of widows, is God in his holy dwelling" (Psalm 68:5).
- "Whoever oppresses the poor shows contempt for their Maker, but whoever is kind to the needy honors God" (Proverbs 14:31).
- "If you spend yourselves in behalf of the hungry and satisfy the needs of the oppressed, then your light will rise in the darkness, and your night will become like the noonday" (Isaiah 58:10).

After Jesus's resurrection and ascension into heaven, the early Christian Church seemed to have a clear grasp on the vital importance of taking care of the needy and less fortunate. In the New Testament, perhaps no one expresses this message for Christians as well as James. He outright states that we are not to merely listen to God's Word but to do what it says (James 1:22). He goes on, though, to make this point incredibly concrete: "Those who consider themselves religious and yet do not keep a tight rein on their tongues deceive themselves, and their religion is worthless. Religion that God our Father accepts as pure and faultless is this: to look after orphans and widows in their distress and to keep oneself from being polluted by the world" (James 1:26–27).

People in those early churches took care of those who were poor and in need, especially the widows and orphans. They served these people not out of duty or political and social obligation but because they loved Jesus. I wonder if some churches today could learn from their example. Too often, it seems that divisive arguments and political posturing have replaced a heart for the poor, the homeless, and the brokenhearted in our society.

A friend of mine who serves a large church here in Nashville shared with me that when his board of elders reaches a stalemate about a budget issue or can't decide how to designate their resources, they've agreed to focus on something very simple and very tangible—helping widows and orphans. My friend explained that keeping their eyes on real people in need right in their own neighborhoods and communities makes it harder to get lost in theological arguments or political agendas. They remember that the answer to "What would Jesus do?" usually has to do with healing, feeding, and serving the people around them.

I've been privileged to help with some special causes that directly support those in need, whether victims of Hurricane Katrina or shelters for domestic abuse victims. Occasionally, fans will find out about these causes and ask me what else they can do besides make a donation. I always tell them to jump into the deep end and find a place to serve in their own communities. To get their hands dirty replacing a roof or serving up soup. To organize a canned food drive for their local church pantry or offer free baby-sitting for a single mom trying to return to work. I encourage them to befriend an older person in a nursing home, to write a thank-you letter to a soldier serving overseas, to purchase and donate sports equipment to a foster home or orphanage. I encourage them to do what Jesus did and ask them to keep challenging me to do the same.

This is how the world will know we are "real country"—by his love.

Conclusion

The Final Touch

My daddy never cared much for religion
And my mama worried a lot about his soul
She'd hit her knees and pray for him on Sunday
While Daddy hit his favorite fishin' hole
You see, Daddy was a rebel and a rambler
But I always knew he loved my mama so
I never doubted he'd make it to heaven
'Cause it's not who you are, it's who ya know
—FROM "JESUS WAS A COUNTRY BOY"

When I wrote the song "Jesus Was a Country Boy," I had no idea of the impact it would have on so many people's lives, including my own. It was one of those songs that I felt great about writing because it expressed my strong opinion on how we all relate to God and how this is distinct from the way organized religion often depicts it. As I've shared throughout these pages, I don't think you have to get dressed up and go to church every week to know God on an intimate level. I'm convinced he reveals himself all around us— in the dappled sunlight falling on a creek bank, in the taste of Mama's fried chicken, in the sound of a child's laughter— if we're only willing to pay attention.

This way of thinking about life isn't something I've made up on my own. What I've tried to share with you is how the life of Jesus reveals that you don't have to be perfect to know God and experience his love. You don't have to get your life together, have perfect kids, live in the right neighborhood, and belong to a certain denomination. You can come just as you are, the way you are. As I mention in the song, it's not who you are—it's Who ya know!

In addition to the amazing example I've found in the life of Jesus, I've been incredibly blessed to have an earthly father who loved me well. I lost him not so long ago, and I still miss him every day. A country boy through and through, he taught me what it means to be a man, both by his words and his actions. We had some precious time together as he approached the end of his time here on Earth, and he shared a few things I'd like to leave with you here as we wrap up our time together.

Word to the Wise

First, Daddy taught me that a man is only as good as his word. If you say you're going to do something, then you better make sure you do it. A country boy doesn't make empty promises or say what people want to hear just to get what he wants in the moment. "Son, it don't matter if you're able to fool all the people all the time because you still got to live with yourself. And you still gotta answer to the good Lord above. He knows what's in your heart even better than you do."

Daddy knew that words carry more power than just the literal meaning of the syllables spoke. He knew that the Bible tells us that God himself is the ultimate Word: "In the beginning was the Word, and the Word was with God, and the Word was God. He was with God in the beginning. Through him all things were made; without him nothing was made that has been made. In him was life, and that life was the light of all mankind. The light shines in the darkness, and the darkness has not overcome it" (John 1:1–5). This light is, of course, his Son, Jesus. "The Word became flesh and made his dwelling among us" (John 1:14).

So often our words determine our actions. What we tell ourselves is often what we believe, let alone what others believe about us. Throughout the Bible, we see that words have incredible power and we're repeatedly told to guard our hearts by guarding what we say. The Psalmist wrote, "Whoever of you loves life and desires to see many good days, keep your tongue from evil and your lips from telling lies" (Psalm 34:12–13). Jesus also made it clear that what we say reflects what's inside us: "What goes into someone's mouth does not defile them, but what comes out of their mouth, that is what defiles them" (Matthew 15:11).

People live and die by their words. The power of your words will shape your life, one way or another. What we say, the words we speak, is often the most important part of who we really are and what we really believe. Therefore, just as my daddy urged me, I encourage you to think about their power in your life. Guard your life with your tongue, or better yet, guard your tongue with your life.

You Can't Outrun the Devil

My daddy also told me something during the last days of his life that has made me laugh and cry and ponder what he meant. It had to do with how we face the hardships of life, the conflicts and the unexpected losses, the disappointments and the disasters, the trials that take us to the edge of despair. As we talked about some of the hardships of his life, my father said, "Son, sometimes you got to face the devil and look him in the eye. You can't outrun that S.O.B.—you can only meet him in the middle of the road head-on!" That's the way my daddy was, plainspoken, honest, and filled with the wisdom of a country boy who's lived a long and heartfelt life.

When it was clear that he had only a few weeks, maybe days, to live, I asked him one day if he was ready to go.

"Yes, I'm ready," he said softly.

"How do you know?" I asked.

"I know I'm ready because I've done my part," he replied. "I've done what God asked me to do."

I didn't push him further because it was clear that the rest was between him and God. But I could tell from the peace in his voice and the glimmer in his eye that he meant what he said.

Shortly after this exchange, Jessie came into the room. She had not seen my dad in such a weakened condition before and began to tear up. But Daddy saw her and said, "No, no, sweetheart—we'll save the tears for last." Sure enough, as I thought about it, I hadn't seen him cry once in the past months leading up to that moment.

I've thought about his words many times since he passed away. As I've turned his advice over in my thoughts, I believe he meant that you have to fight the hard things of life straight up, without trying to pretend otherwise and without allowing them to consume you. As we've seen in the life of Jesus, he certainly squared off with the devil and won the ultimate battle. Not only did he win the showdown in the desert after he'd been fasting for forty days, but Jesus stared death in the eye, tasted it, chewed it up, swallowed it—and then spit it out once and for all.

Jesus gives all of us hope and reminds us that nothing is impossible through the power of God. No matter what you're facing right now—whether it's cancer like my daddy faced, or the betrayal of your spouse, the loss of your job, or a serious illness in your children—you must never give up the good fight. Just do the next thing you know to do. That's what I always saw my daddy do when times were hard. When I was growing up, he didn't always know where the money would come from to fix the truck, but he knew that the garden needed hoeing and the animals needed tending. He just did the next thing he knew to do. He just did his part and obeyed what God asked him to do.

A Wing and a Prayer

Finally, during the last days of his life, Dad reminded me to keep praying. Now, you need to realize that this was from a man who wasn't necessarily what you might think of as the praying type. I can count the times I saw him in church throughout my whole life on both hands. And while we'd give thanks before a big family meal, especially at Thanksgiving and Christmas, we weren't the formal type of folks who had to wait on hearing "Amen!" before we passed the mashed potatoes and turnip greens.

But what I realized over time, and what my father reminded me of there at the end, is that the best prayers come from how we live each day. Did we spend some time outside and recognize the beauty our Creator has placed around us? That's a kind of prayer. Did we catch a big-mouth bass down at the fishin' hole and appreciate the intricate design of creation? That's also a prayer. Did we lend a helping hand to a neighbor who's down on his luck? Or did we sit out on the porch and watch the stars come out, listening to the crickets and frogs sing praise songs from the other side of the holler?

Daddy reminded me that you don't have to stand up in the pulpit of a big church and read an eloquently worded paragraph in a deep, stained-glass voice in order to pray. Every day we have the opportunity to be in conversation with God and to thank him for all the many blessings that he's bestowed on us. We have the opportunity to help those around us and serve them with a smile and a kind word. We get to live another day and know that he's placed us on this Earth for a reason. How we live our lives rings out loud and clear who we are and what we're about, good old country boys and gals trying to make the most of the life we've been given.

When it became clear that my dad was getting close to taking his last breath, I asked him if he wanted to talk to my mother, and he tapped my hand and nodded yes. They had divorced when I was four years old, but he had never remarried, and it had been clear throughout his life that he had never stopped loving her. So I called my mom and put her on speakerphone so that my father could hear her voice one more time.

As she told him that she loved him, big tears ran down his face. He whispered, "I love you, too." They spoke for a few more moments, and the love and forgiveness between them was more than evident. Even in his last few seconds on this earth, my father was still teaching me, still setting an example. It was only a few more hours before he passed away, surrounded by people who loved him—me, my wife, my sister Kimberly.

Daddy lived a life that I believe stayed true to his country-boy roots as well as his love of Jesus. The same kind of life that I aspire to daily. The same kind of life that I wish for you, my friend, as we reach the end of our visit together between these pages.

Jesus sure knew what it meant to be a country boy, and his earthy, honest faith and real, heartfelt love changed the course of time and history. He wasn't some stuck-up preacher or educated elitist snob. He was a guy who liked hanging with the sort of people whom you'd find today down at the corner bar or dancing at the honky-tonk Saturday night, the everyday joes and shady ladies, the fishermen and outcasts. He loved the land and spent more time outdoors than he did inside under a roof.

Jesus calls us to stay in touch with the best parts of being country, too. His example reminds us that family and friends come first. We need to remember to look for signs of our Father's love in everything around us, especially the many beautiful masterpieces he paints outside in the natural world. Yes, Jesus was a country boy, and his life reminds us that no matter where we were born and raised, if we keep our country spirit, our lives will be richer in the things that matter most. As my daddy would say, "Do your part and save the tears for last."

Permissions

★ ★ ★ ★ ★ ★ ★ ★ ★

Join Clay's Fan Club!

★ ★ ★ ★ ★ ★ ★ ★ ★

Readers of the book

Jesus Was a Country Boy

can become members of

Clay's fan club free!

Simply go to

https://www.claywalker.com/fanclub.html

and enter the code CWBOOKFAN